NINOTCHKA

THE MGM LIBRARY OF FILM SCRIPTS

Ninotchka

North by Northwest

Adam's Rib

In preparation:

A Night at the Opera

A Day at the Races

Singin' in the Rain

Ninotchka

A VIKING FILM BOOK

Screenplay by Charles Brackett,
Billy Wilder, and Walter Reisch

NEW YORK / *The Viking Press*

Published in 1972 in a hardbound and
paperbound edition by The Viking Press, Inc.
625 Madison Avenue, New York, N.Y. 10022

Published simultaneously in Canada by
The Macmillan Company of Canada Limited

SBN 670-51404-7 (hardbound)
       670-01932-1 (paperbound)

Library of Congress catalog card number: 78-172942

Printed in U.S.A.

CREDITS

Production	Metro-Goldwyn-Mayer
Produced and directed by	Ernst Lubitsch
Screenplay by	Charles Brackett, Billy Wilder and Walter Reisch
Based on the original story by	Melchior Lengyel
Director of Photography	William Daniels, A.S.C.
Film Editor	Gene Ruggiero
Make-up	Jack Dawn
Hair styles for Miss Claire	Sydney Guilaroff
Time	110 minutes
Released	1939

CAST

NINOTCHKA (Nina Yakushova)	Greta Garbo
COUNT LEON d'ALGOUT	Melvyn Douglas
GRAND DUCHESS SWANA	Ina Claire
MICHAEL IRANOFF	Sig Rumann
BULJANOFF	Felix Bressart
KOPALSKI	Alexander Granach
COMMISSAR RAZININ	Bela Lugosi
COUNT ALEXIS RAKONIN	Gregory Gaye
GASTON	Richard Carle
MERCIER	Edwin Maxwell
HOTEL MANAGER	Rolfe Sedan
RUSSIAN VISA OFFICIAL	George Tobias
SWANA'S MAID, JACQUELINE	Dorothy Adams
GENERAL SAVITZKY	Lawrence Grant
PÈRE MATHIEU, CAFE OWNER	Charles Judels
LAWYER	Frank Reicher
LAWYER	Edwin Stanley

NOTE

Square brackets indicate those parts of the original script that were not filmed; footnotes show important additions in the completed film. Minor variations that do not affect plot or characterization have not been documented.

NINOTCHKA

Fade In on:
An Establishing Shot of Paris in the Month of April[1]

Dissolve to:
The Luxurious Lobby of the Hotel Clarence

CAMERA *moves to a* CLOSE SHOT *of the desk. In the background is a revolving door leading to the street. Through the revolving door comes a strangely dressed individual, obviously one who doesn't belong in such surroundings. It is* COMRADE BULJANOFF, *a member of the Russian Board of Trade. Despite the spring climate of Paris, he still wears his typical Russian clothes, consisting of a coat with a fur collar, a fur cap, and heavy boots.*

BULJANOFF *glances around the lobby, obviously overwhelmed by its magnificence. The* MANAGER, *puzzled by* BULJANOFF's *strange appearance, approaches him.*

MANAGER *(politely)*: Is there anything I can do for you, monsieur?

BULJANOFF: No, no.

He exits toward the street. The MANAGER *returns to his customary duties, when suddenly a second Russian, similarly dressed, pushes his way through the door and gazes around. It is* COMRADE IRANOFF.

The MANAGER, *definitely mystified by now, approaches him.*

MANAGER: Yes, monsieur?

IRANOFF: Just looking around.

---

[1] In the film, there is an extreme long shot of the Place de la Concorde in Paris, with the superimposed title: THIS PICTURE TAKES PLACE IN PARIS IN THOSE WONDERFUL DAYS WHEN A SIREN WAS A BRUNETTE AND NOT AN ALARM . . . AND IF A FRENCHMAN TURNED OUT THE LIGHT IT WAS NOT ON ACCOUNT OF AN AIR RAID!

1

IRANOFF *exits. Again the* MANAGER *returns to his duties, when suddenly he sees that a third man, dressed in the same fashion, has appeared in the revolving door. It is* COMRADE KOPALSKI.

KOPALSKI *doesn't leave the revolving door at all but as it turns, drinks in the whole spectacle of the lobby. The* MANAGER *is by now dumfounded.*

STREET IN FRONT OF THE HOTEL CLARENCE

A taxi stands at the curb. BULJANOFF *and* IRANOFF *are waiting beside it,* IRANOFF *holding a suitcase.* KOPALSKI, *returning from the hotel, joins the group.*

KOPALSKI: Comrades, why should we lie to each other? It's wonderful.[2]

IRANOFF: Let's be honest. Have we anything like it in Russia?

ALL THREE *(agreeing with him)*: No, no, no.

IRANOFF: Can you imagine what the beds would be in a hotel like that?

KOPALSKI: They tell me when you ring once the valet comes in; when you ring twice you get the waiter; and do you know what happens when you ring three times? A maid comes in—a French maid.

IRANOFF *(with a gleam in his eye)*: Comrades, if we ring nine times . . . let's go in.

BULJANOFF *(stopping him)*: Just a minute—just a minute—I have nothing against the idea but I still say let's go back to the Hotel Terminus. Moscow made our reservations there, we are on an official mission, and we have no right to change the orders of our superior.

IRANOFF: Where is your courage, Comrade Buljanoff?

KOPALSKI: Are you the Buljanoff who fought on the barricades? And now you are afraid to take a room with a bath?

BULJANOFF *(stepping back into the taxi)*: I don't want to go to Siberia.

---

[2] In the film, Iranoff and Kopalski start out; Buljanoff stops them.

IRANOFF *and* KOPALSKI *follow him reluctantly.*

IRANOFF: I don't want to go to the Hotel Terminus.

KOPALSKI: If Lenin were alive he would say, "Buljanoff, Comrade, for once in your life you're in Paris. Don't be a fool. Go in there and ring three times."

IRANOFF: He wouldn't say that. What he would say is "Buljanoff, you can't afford to live in a cheap hotel. Doesn't the prestige of the Bolsheviks mean *anything* to you? Do you want to live in a hotel where you press for the hot water and cold water comes and when you press for the cold water nothing comes out at all? Phooey, Buljanoff!"

BULJANOFF *(weakening)*: I still say our place is with the common people, but who am I to contradict Lenin? Let's go in.

All three start to leave the taxi, as we

Dissolve to:

Lobby—Hotel Clarence—at the Desk

BULJANOFF, IRANOFF, *and* KOPALSKI *are approaching the* MANAGER, *their only suitcase carried by two of them.*

KOPALSKI: Are you the manager?

MANAGER *(eyeing the three suspiciously)*: Yes.

KOPALSKI: Pardon me for introducing Comrade Iranoff, member of the Russian Board of Trade.

MANAGER *(bowing with strained politeness)*: Monsieur.

IRANOFF: This is Comrade Kopalski.

MANAGER: Monsieur.

BULJANOFF: I am Comrade Buljanoff.

MANAGER: Monsieur.

BULJANOFF: May I ask how much your rooms are?

MANAGER *(trying to get rid of them)*: Well, gentlemen, I'm afraid our rates are rather high.

[BULJANOFF: Why should *you* be afraid?][3]

---

[3] In the film, Buljanoff says, "Why should you be afraid? Why should he?" They laugh.

The other two nod their agreement. The MANAGER *has noted the single suitcase.*

MANAGER *(haughtily)*: I might be able to accommodate you. Is there some more luggage?

IRANOFF: Oh, yes, but have you a safe here big enough to hold this?

MANAGER: I'm afraid we have no boxes of that size in our vault, but there is one suite with a private safe. . . .

IRANOFF: That's even better.

MANAGER: But, gentlemen, I am afraid . . .

BULJANOFF: He's always afraid.

The other two exchange a look of agreement again.

MANAGER *(a little annoyed)*: I just wanted to explain. The apartment may suit your convenience but I doubt that it will fit your convictions. It's the Royal Suite.

The mention of the Royal Suite startles the three.

BULJANOFF: Royal Suite! *(To the manager)* Just a minute.

The THREE RUSSIANS *take a step away from the manager and go into a huddle.*

BULJANOFF *(in a low voice)*: Now Comrades, I warn you . . . if it gets out in Moscow that we stay in the Royal Suite we will get into terrible trouble.

IRANOFF *(defending his right to a good time)*: We'll just say we had to take it on account of the safe. That's a perfect excuse. There was no other safe big enough.

The other two welcome the suggestion with relish.

BULJANOFF and IRANOFF: That's right. Good, very good.

Suddenly BULJANOFF *grows skeptical again.*

BULJANOFF: Of course, we could take out the pieces and distribute them in three or four boxes in the vault and take a small room. That's an idea, isn't it?

For a moment all three see their bright plans crumble. Then IRANOFF *comes to the rescue.*

IRANOFF: Yes, it's an idea, but who says we have to have an idea?

BULJANOFF *and* KOPALSKI *see the logic of this and their faces light up.*

[BOTH: That's right . . . that's right.][4]

BULJANOFF *(turning to the* MANAGER*)*: Give us the Royal Suite. *The* MANAGER *leads the three toward the elevator.*[5] *The* CAMERA FOLLOWS THEM *and* NARROWS DOWN *to the suitcase carried by two of the* RUSSIANS.

Dissolve to:

Dark Interior of Safe—Royal Suite

We hear from the outside the turning of a key, the opening of a door, then the turning of the dial, and then we see the safe door open. Through the open door we now see the Royal Suite. The THREE RUSSIANS *are standing in front of the safe. One of them puts the suitcase into it.*

Medium Shot—Royal Suite of the Hotel Clarence

Shooting from the interior of the room toward the safe. The THREE RUSSIANS *are standing around it. As* BULJANOFF *and* IRANOFF *close the safe door,* KOPALSKI *walks out of the shot. The* CAMERA STAYS *for a few seconds on* BULJANOFF *and* IRANOFF, *then* PANS OVER *to the center of the room, where a waiter is setting a breakfast table. He is the former* COUNT RAKONIN, *a Russian exile employed by the Hotel Clarence.* RAKONIN *is looking with great interest toward the safe, and as he does so we hear* KOPALSKI'*s voice talking into the telephone.*

KOPALSKI'S VOICE: Will you connect me with Mercier . . . yes, the jeweler. . . .

RAKONIN *pricks up his ears and looks toward the telephone.*

---

[4] In the film, instead, KOPALSKI says, "That's right. That's very good."

[5] In the film, the MANAGER says, "Step this way, please."

Close Shot—Kopalski—at Telephone[6]

KOPALSKI: I want to speak with Monsieur Mercier personally.
. . . Hello, Monsieur Mercier? This is Kopalski of the Russian
Board of Trade. We arrived this morning. . . . Thank you.

Close Shot—Rakonin

*As he sets the breakfast table, his interest in the telephone
conversation increases.*

KOPALSKI'S VOICE: Yes, everything is here. The necklace too. All
fourteen pieces. . . . What? No, Monsieur Mercier, the court
jewels of the Duchess Swana consisted of fourteen pieces. Why
don't you check on that? Naturally, we have all the necessary
credentials.

As the voice continues, we

Dissolve to:
[Service Staircase—Hotel Clarence

RAKONIN *hurries down the stairs, buttoning his overcoat around
him. He exits through a door to the street.*][7]

Wipe to:
Street Corner Near the Hotel Clarence

RAKONIN *is getting into a taxi.*

RAKONIN (*to taxi driver*): Eight Rue de Chalon.

---

[6] In the film, it is IRANOFF on the phone.

[7] In the film, instead of this, the dissolve is to the interior of the Service
Room. RAKONIN enters and approaches another waiter.

RAKONIN: Will you take care of the Royal Suite? I will be back in ten
minutes.

WAITER: All right, Rakonin.

RAKONIN: Thank you very much. Thank you.

Wipe to:
Insert the House Number "8"

above the doorway of a Parisian apartment house. CAMERA
PULLS BACK TO MEDIUM SHOT *of the whole entrance. Into it
is striding a typical Parisian playboy. He is Count Leon
d'Algout.*

Entrance Hall—Swana's Apartment

[*The door is being opened by* SWANA'*s maid.* LEON *enters like
a man thoroughly at home.*
MAID: Good morning, Count.
LEON: Good morning.
MAID: Her Highness is still dressing.
LEON (*as he walks toward Swana's door*): That's all right.][8]

Long Shot—Swana's Room

SWANA *sits at her dressing table in a negligee.* LEON *enters
with the easy air of an old friend. He kisses her lightly.*
SWANA: Hello, Leon!
LEON: Good morning, Swana.
During SWANA'*s long speech he sits down, not paying much
attention to her patter, lights a cigarette, and glances through
a magazine.*
SWANA: It's really a wretched morning . . . wretched. I can't get
myself right. I wanted to look mellow and I look brittle. My face
doesn't compose well . . . all highlights . . . how can I dim myself down, Leon? Suggest something. I am so bored with this face.
I wish I had someone else's face. Whose face would you have if
you had your choice? Oh, well, I guess one gets the face one
deserves.

---

[8] In the film, the maid does not answer the door. LEON opens it himself and
goes right to SWANA's boudoir.

LEON: Your conversation has one marvelous advantage, Swana. However many questions you ask you never expect an answer.
SWANA: Don't you find that restful?[9] . . . Why didn't you come last night?
LEON: Darling, I was busy looking out for your interests.
SWANA: Did you win?
LEON *(enthusiastically)*: We can forget horse racing, roulette, the stock market . . . our worries are over! You remember that platinum watch with the diamond numbers? You will be in a position to give it to me.
SWANA *(with humor)*: Oh, Leon, you are so good to me. *(She kisses him)*
LEON: We can be rich if you say the word. I had dinner with the Guizots last night.
SWANA *(contemptuously)*: Those newspaper people?
LEON: You'd be surprised how many nice people dine with the Guizots.
SWANA: What a gruesome proof of the power of the press!
LEON: Now listen, Swana . . . I sold Monsieur Guizot the idea of publishing your memoirs in the *Gazette Parisienne.* "The Life and Loves of the Grand Duchess Swana of Russia"!
SWANA *(protestingly)*: Oh, Leon!
LEON: Sweetheart, we won't have to bother about our future if you are willing to raffle off your past!
[SWANA: Was it for this that I refused to endorse Dr. Bertrand's Mouthwash? I could have made a little fortune by saying that the Vincent Vacuum Cleaner was the only vacuum cleaner ever used by the Romanoffs . . . and now you want them to smear my life's secrets over the front page of a tabloid?
LEON: I understand how you feel, but there is a limit to every-

---

[9] In the film, at this point, there is additional dialogue:
LEON: Um-hmm.
SWANA: Good morning, darling.
LEON: Good morning.

thing, particularly pride and dignity. They are willing to pay *any* price! They have a circulation of two million!

SWANA: Imagine two million clerks and shop girls peeking into my life for a sou! Think of my lovely life being wrapped around cheese and blood sausages! I can see a big grease spot in the midst of my most intimate moments!

LEON *knows on which note to play for* SWANA'*s benefit.*

LEON: Well, I am the last person to persuade you, but don't do it blindly . . . if this is your decision, you must be prepared to face the consequences. . . . *(With the expression of a man ready to give his all)* I will have to go to work.

SWANA *rises and goes over to* LEON. *His method has been highly successful.*

SWANA: My little Volga boatman! Stop threatening! I don't deserve this. *(Embracing him)* Are you my little Volga boatman?

LEON: Now, Swana . . .

SWANA: First tell me, are you my little Volga boatman?

LEON *(anything to stop her)*: Yes, I'm your little Volga boatman.

SWANA *(walking back to the dressing table)*: Well . . . two million readers . . . I know exactly what they want. Chapter One: "A Childhood behind Golden Bars. Lovely Little Princess Plays with Rasputin's Beard."

LEON *sits down next to her, growing enthusiastic.*

LEON: I've got one chapter Guizot thinks is terrific. "Caviar and Blood." Swana escapes over the ice!

SWANA: A couple of bloodhounds and we have Uncle Tom's Cabin.

LEON *(thinking of another idea)*: Darling, this would be wonderful! Just once . . . weren't you attacked by a Bolshevik?

SWANA *(straining her memory)*: Was I? No . . . not by a Bolshevik!

LEON: Too bad! Brings our price down ten thousand francs!]

There is a knock on the door.

SWANA: Come in.

The MAID *enters.*

9

MAID: Count Rakonin asks the privilege of a few words, Your Highness.

LEON: Count Rakonin?

SWANA: He's a waiter at the Clarence, poor devil. You know him.

LEON: Oh, yes.

SWANA: Tell him I won't be able to see him for a half an hour.

MAID: The Count says if it could be as soon as possible. It is luncheon time and he is just between courses.[10]

The MAID *exits.* SWANA *walks toward the door of the living room.*

Living Room—Swana's Apartment

A charming room, which manages to create a little of the atmosphere of Old Russia. RAKONIN *stands, his overcoat still buttoned about him, waiting nervously.* SWANA *enters, leaving the door ajar.* RAKONIN *approaches her with the respect he would have paid her at the Imperial Court.*

RAKONIN: Your Highness.

SWANA: How do you do, my friend.[11]

RAKONIN: Your Highness, forgive this intrusion, but . . .

SWANA: What is it, Rakonin? Did you lose your job?

RAKONIN: No, madame, something of the utmost importance . . . it concerns your jewels.

SWANA: My jewels?!

RAKONIN: I remember one birthday of His Majesty, our beloved Czar. . . . I had the honor of being on guard at the summer

---

[10] In the film, SWANA says, "All right, all right. I'll see him right away. But I can't get myself right today!"
LEON and SWANA are sitting by the dressing table. SWANA rises, kisses him, and starts out in the background.
SWANA: Highlights . . .
LEON: Darling, Count Rakonin's between courses.
SWANA: Oh, yes. My little Volga boatman!
LEON: Ummm.
[11] In the film, she adds, "Won't you sit down?"

palace. . . . I still see you bending before His Majesty. . . . You wore your diadem and a necklace . . . [your face seemed to be lighted by the jewels.]

SWANA *(puzzled)*: Why do you bring this up after so many years?

RAKONIN: They are here! . . . Your jewels! . . . Here in Paris!

SWANA: Alexis! Do you know what you are saying?

(See film still 1.)

RAKONIN: This morning three Soviet agents arrived. I overheard a telephone conversation with Mercier, the jeweler. Your Highness, they are going to sell them!

Medium Shot—Door of Bedroom

From the door of the bedroom appears LEON, *his face alert.*

LEON: Did I hear something about jewels?

SWANA: Rakonin, bless him, has given me the most amazing news![12]

Medium Close—Swana and Rakonin

SWANA *goes to the telephone.*

SWANA *(into phone)*: Balzac 2769. . . . *(to* LEON*)* My lawyer . . .

LEON *steps to her side, highly interested.*

RAKONIN: I am sorry . . . I have to leave.

SWANA *(to* RAKONIN*)*: Thank you so much, my friend. I will get in touch with you.

COUNT RAKONIN *leaves.*

SWANA *(into phone)*: This is the Duchess Swana[13] . . . I want to speak to Monsieur Cornillon . . . it's very important . . . please get him right away. . . . Hello, Monsieur Cornillon? The

---

[12] In the film, speaking to RAKONIN, she continues, "You know Count d'Algout."
RAKONIN: How do you do, monsieur.

[13] Throughout the film, she is the *Grand* Duchess Swana.

most incredible thing has happened! My jewels are here in Paris! Three Bolshevik swine are trying to sell them! Yes . . . yes . . . we must act immediately! . . . Call the police. . . . Have them arrested! . . . Well, then, get an injunction! . . . But do something, Monsieur Cornillon! *(Apparently the answer is some objection from* CORNILLON) . . . But they are my jewels! There must be some way of getting them back!

LEON *(just as nervous as* SWANA): What does he say?

SWANA *(to* LEON): Shhh! *(Into phone)* . . . But how can there be a question? . . . Are you my lawyer or theirs? . . . All right, I'll let you know!

> *She hangs up, rises, the legal situation whirling around in her brain.*

LEON: What did he say?

SWANA *(discouraged)*: It looks pretty hopeless . . . there may be a chance . . . that's all. . . . The French Government has recognized Soviet Russia and he doubts that they will risk a war for my poor sake. He might be able to make up some kind of a case but it would cost money, money, *money!* . . . That's all they are interested in—those lawyers!

> *(See film still 2.)*

LEON *(taking her in his arms)*: Darling, calm down. Why do you need a lawyer? Haven't you your little Volga boatman?

> SWANA *looks up at him, hope dawning in her eyes, as we*

Dissolve to:
Insert of the Jewels

> *spread out on a table in the Royal Suite.* CAMERA PULLS BACK *to a* LONGER SHOT. *We see* MERCIER, *the jeweler, examining the jewels with an eyepiece screwed in his eye. Around him stand the* THREE RUSSIANS. MERCIER, *a middle-aged man of the greatest suavity and elegance, but a shrewd trader none the less, looks up.*

MERCIER: Very good . . . superb . . . excellent . . . it would be foolish to belittle the quality of the merchandise but your terms are impossible. My counteroffer is the absolute maximum.

(See film still 3.)

KOPALSKI: But, Monsieur Mercier . . .

MERCIER *(continuing)*: Gentlemen, I'll let you in on a little secret . . . we are only undertaking this deal for the prestige involved, and, quite frankly, we are expecting to take a loss.

IRANOFF *draws* BULJANOFF *aside and whispers in his ear.*

IRANOFF *(whispering)*: Capitalistic methods . . .

BULJANOFF: They accumulate millions by taking loss after loss.

The telephone rings.

BULJANOFF *(answering phone)*: Hello . . . this is Buljanoff, Iranoff, and Kopalski. . . . Who? . . . Count d'Algout? . . . No, no . . . it must be a mistake . . . we can't be disturbed.

MERCIER *(continuing)*: I assure you no one else could meet the figure named by my syndicate . . . at least under the present economic conditions.

KOPALSKI: We can wait.

IRANOFF *(pompously)*: Do we give the impression of people who are pressed for money?

MERCIER: Yes. Gentlemen . . . let's put our cards face down. Right now there is a Russian commission in New York trying to sell fifteen Rembrandts. There is another in London mortgaging the oil fields in Baku. You need money and you need it quickly. I think my offer is fair and does not even take advantage of your situation.

Close-up—Buljanoff, Iranoff, and Kopalski

KOPALSKI *(to* MERCIER*)*: Just a minute.[14]

The THREE RUSSIANS *step to one side.*

[14] In the film, there is this additional exchange:
IRANOFF: Now, listen . . .
BULJANOFF: Wait—just a minute. The pieces are all registered.
MERCIER: Yes, I know. Thank you so much.

IRANOFF (*in a low voice*): He's cutting our throat . . .

BULJANOFF: But what can we do? . . . We have to accept.

KOPALSKI: Comrades! Comrades! Don't let's give in so quickly. After all we have to uphold the prestige of Russia.

BULJANOFF: All right, let's uphold it for another ten minutes.

Shot of the Whole Group

> *There is a knock at the door.* IRANOFF *walks toward it, unlocks it, opens it a little. In the door appears* LEON.

IRANOFF: We don't want to be disturbed.

LEON: My name is Count d'Algout. I telephoned.

IRANOFF: If you want to see us you must come later.

LEON: I just want a word with Monsieur Mercier.

IRANOFF: But you can't . . .

> LEON *pushes his way in. He approaches* MONSIEUR MERCIER. *The* RUSSIANS *get between him and the jewels and during the following scene put them back into the safe.*

LEON: Monsieur Mercier. May I introduce myself? I am Count Leon d'Algout. I think I had the pleasure of meeting you in your beautiful shop. I was admiring a platinum watch with diamond numbers.

MERCIER: Oh, yes, yes . . .

LEON (*glancing at the jewels*): Glorious, aren't they?

KOPALSKI: Now, monsieur, you have no right . . .[15]

LEON (*very charmingly*): Just a moment. (*To* MERCIER) I hope you haven't closed this deal, Monsieur Mercier. It might bring you into serious difficulties.

ALL THREE RUSSIANS: Who are you? What do you want? What is this?

LEON: These jewels are the property of the Duchess Swana of Russia, and were seized illegally by the Soviet Government. I am acting for Her Highness, the Duchess. Here is my power of attorney.

---

[15] In the film, IRANOFF says, "I did not permit you to come in here."

14

He hands it to MERCIER, *who reads it.*

IRANOFF *(excitedly)*: You know, Monsieur Mercier, this is all non-sense.

KOPALSKI: These may have been the jewels of the Duchess Swana, but, like all private property, they were confiscated by the State.

LEON: We'll leave the problem of their ownership to the French courts. Meanwhile I have filed a petition for an injunction to pro-hibit you from either selling or removing the jewels. Here is a copy.[16]

The RUSSIANS *take the copy of the injunction, read it flabber-gasted. As they do so,* LEON *turns to* MONSIEUR MERCIER.

[LEON: I thought it my duty to warn you. I would hate to see you get in any trouble, monsieur.]

MERCIER: Thank you. *(He turns to the* RUSSIANS*)* Gentlemen, this introduces a new element into our negotiations. Until this claim is completely settled . . .

KOPALSKI: We can call our ambassador.

IRANOFF: I give you my word! They were confiscated legally![17]

MERCIER: Please try to understand my position. I am not with-drawing. My offer stands and as soon as you produce a clear title, approved by the French courts, the deal is settled. Until then, good day.

He bows and starts toward the door. LEON *accompanies him, opening the door as though he were the host.*[18]

LEON *(intimately)*: I hope you will forgive me, Monsieur Mercier.

MERCIER *(in a low voice)*: On the contrary. I consider myself very lucky. Good day.

He bows.

---

[16] In the film, LEON continues, "If there is anything in the petition which isn't clear, gentlemen, I shall be glad to explain it."

[17] In the film, KOPALSKI and BULJANOFF ad lib, "That's right! That's right!"

[18] In the film:

LEON: I thought it my duty to warn you. I should have hated to see you get into trouble, m'sieur.

MERCIER: Thank you. Thank you.

LEON (*bowing*): Good day, monsieur.[19]

MERCIER *leaves.* LEON *closes the door and turns back into the room to the three outraged* RUSSIANS.

LEON (*jauntily*): Well, gentlemen . . . how about a little lunch?

IRANOFF: Get out of here!

LEON: Don't look so gloomy, gentlemen. All is not lost. You may have a chance.

KOPALSKI (*bursting forth*): We may have a chance.

LEON: Yes . . . a very slim one. I want to be fair. I don't deny that you might make out some kind of a case.

KOPALSKI: We haven't anything to discuss with you. We'll talk to a lawyer!

LEON: All right—go ahead . . . you talk to the lawyer and I'll talk to the judge!

(See film still 4.)

IRANOFF: That won't help you! You can't intimidate us!

KOPALSKI: Soviet Russia will put all its might behind this case.

BULJANOFF: You think because you represent the former Duchess . . .

LEON: *The* Duchess . . .

BULJANOFF: The *former* Duchess!

LEON: In any case, gentlemen, a charming, beautiful, exquisite woman. I warn you, if this case comes to trial it will be before a French court, and when the Duchess takes the stand . . .

IRANOFF: All right, go ahead, get her on the witness stand! What can she say?

LEON: But how will she look? The fashions this spring are very becoming to her. Gentlemen, the judge will be French, the jury will be French, everybody in that courtroom will be French. Have you ever seen a French court when a beautiful woman sits on the witness stand and lifts her skirt a little? You sit down and pull up your pants and where will it get you?

---

[19] In the film, BULJANOFF says, "You believe me, I—"

16

IRANOFF: I suppose you expect us to hand over the jewels?
LEON: Oh, no, no. I am not a highwayman, I'm just a nuisance. All I'm trying to do is make things as difficult as possible.
BULJANOFF: Not that we are giving in one inch, but tell us . . . what is in your mind?
LEON: Well, gentlemen, how about my proposition?
IRANOFF: What proposition?
LEON: I just said let's have a little lunch. *(Picking up the telephone)* Room service.

Dissolve to:

Medium Shot—Corridor of the Hotel Clarence, *shooting toward door leading to the Royal Suite. Two waiters are wheeling in a table on which is a block of ice filled with caviar and a collection of the most delicious hors d'oeuvres. They enter the room. After the door is closed we hear from within loud* SOUNDS *of approval from* BULJANOFF, IRANOFF, *and* KOPALSKI. *The* CAMERA STAYS *on the door. After a few seconds a very good-looking cigarette girl enters the room and from within we* HEAR *even louder* SOUNDS *of approval. Next a waiter enters carrying champagne and another with glasses on a tray. As they are going into the room, the cigarette girl comes out and runs excitedly down the corridor.* CAMERA PANS *with her away from the door as she starts down the staircase.*

Medium Shot—Door of the Royal Suite
Some of the waiters come out, others go in, carrying further delicacies.

Medium Shot—Head of Staircase
Up the staircase pants the cigarette girl, followed by two other cigarette girls. CAMERA PANS *with them as they rush*

17

toward the door of the Royal Suite and enter. From within
we HEAR *terrific greetings. The* CAMERA REMAINS ON THE
DOOR *as we* SLOWLY DISSOLVE INTO EVENING.

The electric lights are lit and a band of five Hungarian
musicians enters carrying typical Hungarian instruments, in-
cluding a cimbalom.

Long Shot—Royal Suite

The orchestra is playing; the THREE RUSSIANS, *very high*
by now, are dancing with the girls. One of them is wearing the
cigarette tray of one of the girls. It is a harmless but loud and
hilarious party. Apart from all the hullabaloo sits LEON *at the*
desk, a telegraph blank before him.

LEON: Hey, Sascha! Serge! Misha!

The three come to him, all in the gayest, most agreeable mood.

KOPALSKI: Yes, Leon . . .

IRANOFF *(pawing him)*: What is it, my boy?

LEON: About this telegram to Moscow. Why should you bother?
I'll write it for you.

BULJANOFF: Leon . . . Leonitchka . . . *(He embraces* LEON*)*
Why are you so good to us? *(He kisses* LEON*)*

IRANOFF *(kissing* LEON *too)*: Leon, my little boy.

KOPALSKI *(joining them)*: Oh, Leon, you are so good.

LEON *(freeing himself as best he can)*:[20] What's the name of that
Commissar on the Board of Trade?

IRANOFF: Razinin.

LEON *(writing)*: Razinin, Board of Trade, Moscow.

KOPALSKI: You wouldn't like Razinin.

BULJANOFF: He's a bad man. Sends people to Siberia!

IRANOFF: We don't like Razinin.

---

[20] In the film, LEON tries to quiet them first: "That's very nice, boys. Now,
wait a minute—wait a minute, boys— wait a minute."

18

BULJANOFF *(again pawing* LEON*)*: We like you, Leon—don't we like Leon?

The others join him and kiss LEON.

(See film still 5.)

IRANOFF and KOPALSKI: Yes, we like Leon . . . little Leonitchka.

This brings on a new frenzy of Russian affection. LEON *frees himself and rises.*

LEON: How does this strike you? COMMISSAR RAZININ, BOARD OF TRADE, MOSCOW. UNEXPECTED SITUATION HERE. DUCHESS SWANA IN PARIS CLAIMS JEWELS, AND HAS ALREADY BROUGHT INJUNCTION AGAINST SALE OR REMOVAL. AFTER LONG AND CAREFUL STUDY WE SUGGEST IN THE INTEREST OF OUR BELOVED COUNTRY A FIFTY-FIFTY SETTLEMENT AS BEST SOLUTION. IRANOFF, BULJANOFF, AND KOPALSKI.

KOPALSKI: If we say that, Leon . . . we'll be sent to Siberia!

IRANOFF: And if we have to go to Siberia . . .

LEON *(still looking over the telegram)*: I'll send you a muff.

BULJANOFF: Oh, why are you so good to us?

IRANOFF and KOPALSKI: Yes, you are so good, Leon.

Again they overwhelm LEON *with an avalanche of Russian affection. At this moment* RAKONIN *enters with some new bottles of champagne. The* RUSSIANS *immediately leave* LEON *and direct their affection toward* RAKONIN, *embracing and kissing him.*

ALL THREE RUSSIANS: Comrade waiter, dear waiteritchka! . . . Why are you so good to us? You good waiter![21]

After RAKONIN *has turned over the champagne to the* RUSSIANS, LEON *takes him aside.*

LEON: Take this telegram to the telegraph office at once!

RAKONIN: Yes, monsieur.

He leaves the room.

---

[21] In the film, LEON says, "That's enough. Get back to the other room. Enough—enough—go along.

[Close Shot—Door Leading to Corridor of Hotel Clarence

RAKONIN *comes out with the telegram. The* CAMERA PANS *with him as he hurries down the corridor, reading it. The* CAMERA NARROWS DOWN *on an insert of the telegram as we*

Dissolve to:

Telegraph Wires over a Wide Sweep of Country

Dissolve to:

Telegraph Wires over the Roofs of Moscow

PAN *down past the roof of an official building to a* CLOSE SHOT *of a window. Behind it stands* RAZININ, *reading the telegram. He is a violent, militant Bolshevik.*

The telegram fills him with rage. As he crumples it, and stares into space, his expression bodes ill for BULJANOFF, IRANOFF, *and* KOPALSKI.

Fade out

Fade in:

Medium Shot—Upper Corridor of Hotel Clarence, *shooting toward door of elevator. The elevator comes up and stops, the door opens, and the* THREE RUSSIANS *step out. They are very smartly dressed and look like any urbane gentlemen coming from the races. Two of them have racing glasses. As they walk toward the Royal Suite,* LADY LAVENHAM, *an elderly English aristocrat, comes out of her room.*

LADY LAVENHAM: Good afternoon, messieurs, *mes* Comrades.

ALL THREE RUSSIANS: Good afternoon, Lady Lavenham.

KOPALSKI: And how is Lord Lavenham?

BULJANOFF: . . . and little Lady Beatrice?

20

LADY LAVENHAM: Very well. Did fortune favor you at the races?

IRANOFF: Comme ci, comme ca.

LADY LAVENHAM: I understand . . . nothing to write home about.

BULJANOFF *(alarmed)*: Who wants to write home about it?

LADY LAVENHAM: It's just a saying. How about joining us Saturday night for dinner? We're having a few friends.

KOPALSKI: Are we free, Buljanoff?

BULJANOFF: Possibly.

IRANOFF: We'll manage.

LADY LAVENHAM: Then let's say at nine.

BULJANOFF: Black tie or white tie?

LADY LAVENHAM: Oh, let's make it white.

BULJANOFF: Certainly!

LADY LAVENHAM: *Au revoir.*

ALL THREE RUSSIANS: *Au revoir.*

As they walk into the Royal Suite, BULJANOFF *tosses off an urbane comment.*

BULJANOFF: Nice people.]

Anteroom of Royal Suite

As the three enter, the telephone rings. BULJANOFF *and* KO-PALSKI *go into the living room.* IRANOFF *answers the telephone.*

IRANOFF *(into telephone)*: Yes, Leon . . . *(A little bit annoyed)* What is it, Leon? . . . You can't hurry such things. . . . You must give Moscow a little time. . . . There's nothing we can do about it . . . why don't you drop in later? . . . *Au revoir.* . . .

He steps into the living room.

Living Room

As IRANOFF *enters* BULJANOFF *rushes toward him.*

BULJANOFF: Misha! Misha!

IRANOFF: What is it?

21

BULJANOFF: A telegram from Moscow! It must have been here all day!

KOPALSKI *(joining them and reading telegram)*: HALT NEGOTIATIONS IMMEDIATELY. ENVOY EXTRAORDINARY ARRIVES THURSDAY SIX TEN WITH FULL POWER. YOUR AUTHORITY CANCELLED HEREWITH. RAZININ.

IRANOFF: It *is* Thursday!

BULJANOFF: It's six o'clock already!

They rush into the bedroom.

KOPALSKI: I always said it would be Siberia!

Dissolve to:

[Lobby—Hotel Clarence

MANAGER *at desk*. IRANOFF, BULJANOFF, AND KOPALSKI *rush from the direction of the elevator*. IRANOFF *pauses at the desk. The others go on to the door and wait for him there.*

IRANOFF *(to MANAGER)*: A Special Envoy is coming from Moscow. He'll occupy the Royal Suite. Move our things to the smallest room you've got.

MANAGER: Yes, monsieur.

IRANOFF: Right away . . . instantly!

From the door BULJANOFF *and* KOPALSKI *call impatiently.*

BULJANOFF and KOPALSKI: Iranoff!

IRANOFF: I'm coming!

As he starts toward the door, we][22]

Dissolve to:

Platform—Paris Railroad Station

The train has already arrived as the THREE RUSSIANS *hurry down the platform. Neither do they know the name of the*

---

[22] Instead, in the film, IRANOFF is on the phone: "Come on. Give me the desk, please. This . . . this is the Royal Suite. Iranoff speaking. Listen, a special envoy is coming from Moscow today. He'll occupy the Royal Suite. Move our things to the smallest room you've got. Yes, right away! Instantly!"

Envoy Extraordinary, nor his appearance, and they are search-
ing the crowd for some clue.

IRANOFF: This is a fine thing. Maybe we've missed him
already.

KOPALSKI: How can you find somebody without knowing what
he looks like?

IRANOFF points to a bearded man with a knapsack.

IRANOFF: That must be the one!

BULJANOFF: Yes, he looks like a comrade!

They follow the man, but just as they are ready to approach
him he is greeted by a German GIRL. Both raise their hands
in the Nazi salute.

BEARDED MAN and GIRL: Heil Hitler!

As the two embrace, the THREE RUSSIANS stop in their
tracks.

KOPALSKI: No, that's not him. . . .

BULJANOFF: Positively not!

By now the platform is almost empty. As the RUSSIANS in
the foreground look around helplessly, we see in the back-
ground a woman who obviously is also looking for someone.
It is NINOTCHKA YAKUSHOVA, the Envoy Extraordinary. The
RUSSIANS exchange troubled looks and go toward her. NI-
NOTCHKA comes forward. As they meet she speaks.

NINOTCHKA *(to* IRANOFF*)*: I am looking for Michael Simonovitch
Iranoff.

IRANOFF: I am Michael Simonovitch Iranoff.

NINOTCHKA: I am Nina Ivanovna Yakushova, Envoy Extraordinary, acting under direct orders of Comrade Commissar Razinin.
Present me to your colleagues.

They shake hands. NINOTCHKA's grip is strong as a man's.

IRANOFF: Comrade Buljanoff . . .

NINOTCHKA: Comrade.

IRANOFF: Comrade Kopalski . . .

NINOTCHKA: Comrade.

23

IRANOFF: What a charming idea for Moscow to surprise us with a lady comrade.

KOPALSKI: If we had known we would have greeted you with flowers.

NINOTCHKA *(sternly)*: Don't make an issue of my womanhood. We are here for work . . . all of us. Let's not waste time. Shall we go?

> The RUSSIANS *are taken aback. As* NINOTCHKA *bends down to lift her two suitcases,* IRANOFF *calls:*

IRANOFF: Porter!

> *A* PORTER *steps up to them.*

PORTER: Here, please . . .

NINOTCHKA: What do you want?

PORTER: May I have your bags, madame?

NINOTCHKA: Why?

KOPALSKI: He is a porter. He wants to carry them.

NINOTCHKA *(to* PORTER): Why? . . . Why should you carry other people's bags?

PORTER: Well . . . that's my business, madame.

NINOTCHKA: That's no business . . . that's a social injustice.

PORTER: That depends on the tip.

KOPALSKI *(trying to take* NINOTCHKA'S *bags)*: Allow me, Comrade.

NINOTCHKA: No, thank you.

> NINOTCHKA *takes both suitcases and walks away with the* THREE RUSSIANS, *whose nervousness has increased with every word from the Envoy Extraordinary.*

BULJANOFF: How are things in Moscow?

NINOTCHKA: Very good. The last mass trials were a great success. There are going to be fewer but better Russians.

> *The hearts of the* THREE RUSSIANS *drop to their boots, as we*

Dissolve to:

Lobby—Hotel Clarence

> NINOTCHKA, *followed by the* RUSSIANS, *comes through the lobby, observing every detail of these unfamiliar surroundings.*

24

Suddenly she stops. In the showcase of a hat shop in the lobby is displayed a hat of the John-Frederic's type.

NINOTCHKA: What's that?

KOPALSKI: It's a hat, Comrade, a woman's hat.

NINOTCHKA shakes her head.

NINOTCHKA: Tsk, tsk, tsk, how can such a civilization survive which permits women to put things like that on their heads. It won't be long now, Comrades.

She walks out of the shot toward the elevator, followed by the THREE RUSSIANS, as we

Dissolve to:

Royal Suite

NINOTCHKA *enters, followed by the* THREE RUSSIANS, *who by now are frightened to death.*

BULJANOFF: This is the apartment we have reserved for you, Comrade Yakushova. I hope you like it.

NINOTCHKA *(glancing around the tremendous room)*: Which part of the room is mine?

(See film still 6.)

IRANOFF: You see . . . it is a little different here. They don't rent rooms in pieces. We had to take the whole suite.

NINOTCHKA *begins to unpack her things and puts her typewriter on the desk.*

NINOTCHKA: How much does this cost?

IRANOFF: Two thousand francs.

NINOTCHKA: A week?

IRANOFF: A day.

NINOTCHKA: Do you know how much a cow costs, Comrade Iranoff?

IRANOFF: A cow?

NINOTCHKA: Two thousand francs. If I stay here a week I will cost the Russian people seven cows. *(With an outburst of emotion)* Who am I to cost the Russian people seven cows?

BULJANOFF: We had to take it on account of the safe.

IRANOFF: For ourselves . . . we are much happier now since we moved to a little room next to the servants' quarters.

NINOTCHKA *takes Lenin's picture from her bags.*
(See film still 7.)

NINOTCHKA: I am ashamed to put the picture of Lenin in a room like this. *(She puts the photograph on the desk)*[23] Comrades, your telegram was received with great disfavor in Moscow.

KOPALSKI: We did our best, Comrade.

NINOTCHKA: I hope so for your sake. *(She sits at her desk and starts to type her report)*: Let us examine the case. What does the lawyer say?

BULJANOFF: Which lawyer?

NINOTCHKA: You didn't get legal advice?

[BULJANOFF: We didn't want to get mixed up with lawyers. They are very expensive here. If you just say hello to a lawyer . . . well, there goes another cow.]

KOPALSKI: We dealt directly with the representative of the Grand Duchess. I am sure if we call him he will give you a very clear picture.

NINOTCHKA: I will not repeat your mistake. I will have no dealings with the Grand Duchess nor her representative.

NINOTCHKA *continues to type. The* THREE RUSSIANS *watch her nervously. Each click pounds on their consciences.*

NINOTCHKA *(looking up)*: Comrade Buljanoff . . .

BULJANOFF: Yes, Comrade?

NINOTCHKA: Do you spell Buljanoff with one or two f's?

BULJANOFF *(with fright in his voice)*: With two f's, if you please.

NINOTCHKA *goes on with her typing. Suddenly she looks up at* IRANOFF, *who becomes self-conscious and fixes his tie. As he does so he sees that* NINOTCHKA's *glance is concentrated on*

---

[23] In the film:
IRANOFF: Do you want to be alone, Comrade?
NINOTCHKA: No.

the spats which he was wearing and in his hurry forgot to remove. He knows it is too late to do anything about it except to stand one foot behind the other, as NINOTCHKA *types faster, the clicking of her keys twice as loud.* [NINOTCHKA *picks up the telephone.*

NINOTCHKA *(into phone)*: Will you send me some cigarettes, please?][24] *(Suddenly getting up)* Comrades, I am not in a position to pass final judgment but at best you have been careless in your duty to the State. *(With utmost gravity)* You were entrusted with more than a mere sale of jewelry. Why are we peddling our precious possessions to the world at this time? Our next year's crop is in danger and you know it. Unless we can get foreign currency to buy tractors there will not be enough bread for our people. And you three comrades. . . .

KOPALSKI: We did it with the best intentions. . . .

NINOTCHKA: We cannot feed the Russian people on your intentions. Fifty per cent to a so-called Duchess! . . . Half of every loaf of bread to our enemy! Comrade Kopalski, go at once to our Embassy and get the address of the best lawyer in Paris.

KOPALSKI: Yes, Comrade.

NINOTCHKA: You, Comrade Iranoff, go to the Public Library and get me the section of the Civil Code on property.

BULJANOFF: Is there anything I can do, Comrade?

NINOTCHKA: You might get me an accurate map of Paris. I want to use my spare time to inspect the public utilities and make a study of all outstanding technical achievements in the city.

BULJANOFF: Yes, Comrade.

The buzzer rings.

---

[24] In the film, instead:
NINOTCHKA: Have you some cigarettes?
IRANOFF, BULJANOFF, and KOPALSKI go through their pockets. IRANOFF picks up the telephone.
IRANOFF: This is the Royal Suite. Please send up some cigarettes. Yes. (To NINOTCHKA) You just telephone and you get what you want. That's the capitalistic system.

NINOTCHKA: Come in.

The three CIGARETTE GIRLS *enter.*

CIGARETTE GIRLS *(gaily)*: Hello! Hello! Cigarettes?

NINOTCHKA *looks up astonished. Seeing her, the* CIGARETTE GIRLS *freeze. The* RUSSIANS *stand by quietly.*

NINOTCHKA *(looking at the* RUSSIANS*)*: Comrades, you seem to have been smoking a lot.

Fade out

Fade in:

Medium Shot—Lobby—Hotel Clarence—Evening, *shooting past the desk toward the revolving door. The telephone rings and the* DESK CLERK *answers.*

DESK CLERK: Desk . . . yes, Monsieur Kopalski . . . *(he writes down the message)* . . . you are expecting Count d'Algout . . . uh huh . . . but he is not to go to the Royal Suite under any circumstances. He should go to your new room, 985? Thank you, monsieur. *(he hangs up the receiver)*

[*A few seconds later* NINOTCHKA, *naturally completely unaware of the telephone conversation, passes by. She carries a map in her hand.*

DESK CLERK: Good evening, madame.

NINOTCHKA: Good evening.

She exits out the door.]

Exterior, Hotel Clarence

NINOTCHKA *emerges,* [*unfolds the map.*

Close-up—Map of Paris

in the hands of Ninotchka. The CAMERA ZOOMS *down to a* CLOSE-UP *of the little drawing of the Hotel Clarence on the* map. *The* CAMERA *then* PANS OVER *from the Clarence toward the opposite side of the street, but before we reach the opposite side we see that in the center of the street is a little isle of safety. The* CAMERA *proceeds* PANNING *to the opposite side of the square and we*

Dissolve to:

The Real Location Corresponding to That Seen on the Map

and seen from the same ANGLE.] *It is evening, and along the street comes* LEON *on his way to the hotel. The* CAMERA PANS *with him as he crosses the street. He reaches the isle of safety and there passes* NINOTCHKA, *who has come from the other side. They pass on the little isle without noticing each other. Suddenly we hear the whistle of a traffic policeman and both* NINOTCHKA *and* LEON *have to step back to the little isle.*

Close Shot—Ninotchka and Leon

on the little isle. Wanting some information NINOTCHKA *turns to him—completely impersonal.*

NINOTCHKA: You, please.

LEON: Me?

NINOTCHKA: Yes. Could you give me some information?

LEON: Gladly.[25]

NINOTCHKA: How long do we have to wait here?

LEON: Well—until the policeman whistles again.

NINOTCHKA: At what intervals does he whistle?

LEON: What?

NINOTCHKA: How many minutes between the first and second whistle?

LEON: That's funny. It's interesting. I never gave it a thought before.

[25] In the film, NINOTCHKA takes out her map and unfolds it; LEON helps.

29

NINOTCHKA: Have you never been caught in a similar situation?
LEON: Have I? Do you know when I come to think about it it's staggering. If I add it all up I must have spent years waiting for signals. Imagine! An important part of my life wasted between whistles.
NINOTCHKA: In other words you don't know.
LEON: No.
NINOTCHKA: Thank you.
LEON: You're welcome.

[NINOTCHKA *gets out her map, starts to unfold it.*]

LEON: Can I help you?
NINOTCHKA: You might hold this for me.
LEON: Love to.
NINOTCHKA *(engrossed in her geography)*: Correct me if I am wrong. . . . We are facing north, aren't we?
LEON *(bewildered)*: Facing north. . . . I'd hate to commit myself without my compass. . . . Pardon me . . . are you an explorer?
(See film still 8.)
NINOTCHKA: No . . . I am looking for the Eiffel Tower.
LEON: Is that thing lost again? . . . Listen . . . if you are interested in a view . . .
NINOTCHKA: I am interested in the Eiffel Tower from a technical standpoint.
LEON: Technical . . . I couldn't help you from that angle. You see, a real Parisian only goes to the top of the tower in moments of despair to jump off.
NINOTCHKA: How long does it take a man to land?
LEON: Now, isn't that too bad! The last time I jumped I forgot to clock it! *(Looks at map)* Let me see . . . Eiffel Tower. . . . Your finger, please.
He takes her finger and points to the map with it.
NINOTCHKA *(skeptically)*: Why do you need my finger?
LEON: Bad manners to point with your own. . . . Here . . . the Eiffel Tower.

NINOTCHKA: And where are *we*?

LEON *(shifting her finger back to the hotel)*: Here . . . here we are . . . here you are and here I am . . . feel it?

NINOTCHKA: I am interested only in the shortest distance between these two points. Must you flirt?

LEON: I don't have to but I find it natural.

NINOTCHKA: Suppress it.

LEON: I'll try.

> NINOTCHKA *starts to fold her map.*

NINOTCHKA: For my own information would you call your approach toward me typical of the local morale?

LEON: Madame, it is that kind of approach which has made Paris what it is.

NINOTCHKA: You are very sure of yourself, aren't you?

LEON: Nothing has occurred recently to shake my confidence.

NINOTCHKA: I have heard of the arrogant male in capitalistic society. It is having a superior earning power that makes you like that.

LEON: A *Russian*! I *love* Russians! Comrade . . . I have been fascinated by your Five-Year Plan for the past fifteen years!

NINOTCHKA: Your type will soon be extinct.

> *She walks away from him coldly.* LEON *stares after her, fascinated.*[26]

Dissolve to:

Entrance—Ground Floor of the Eiffel Tower

> CAMERA *moves with* NINOTCHKA *as she enters. She approaches an* ATTENDANT.

NINOTCHKA: Please . . . can you tell me the exact width of the foundation on which the piers are resting? . . . and the depth?

ATTENDANT: You don't have to worry. The thing is safe.

---

[26] In the film, LEON calls a taxi.

NINOTCHKA: I am not afraid . . . I want to know . . .

LEON, *who apparently has taken a taxi and prepared himself otherwise, enters the scene, reading from a book.*

LEON *(reading)*: The foundation is one hundred and forty-one yards square. . . . *(He tips his hat and interjects)* I hope you'll forgive me but I thought you'd . . .

NINOTCHKA *(interrupting)*: Go ahead.

The CAMERA *goes with* NINOTCHKA *and* LEON *as they walk toward the steps.*

LEON *(continuing)*: Four massive piers of masonry are sunk to a depth of forty-six feet on the side of the Seine, and twenty-nine and one-half feet on the other side. The girders of interlaced ironwork which stay the structure have an inclination of fifty-four degrees. . . .

NINOTCHKA: That's a strange angle.

LEON: Yes, very strange.

By now they have reached the staircase. They start up.

LEON *(continuing to read)*: Ascending to the tower is a staircase consisting of eight hundred and twenty-nine steps . . . *(This disclosure frightens* LEON *as he realizes the climb ahead of him. He reads on as they walk up)* . . . and an additional two hundred and fifty-four steps to the very top. . . . *(Now* LEON *stops but* NINOTCHKA *proceeds on out of the picture.* LEON *calls after her and reads from his book in a loud voice)* There is an elevator included in the price of admission!

NINOTCHKA *continues to climb.*[27]

Medium Shot—Stairs (from Leon's Angle)

NINOTCHKA, *paying no attention to him, walks up the stairs, two at a time.*

---

[27] In the film, LEON continues, "It'll take you hours to walk up there. The elevator will get you up in three minutes."

Close Shot—Leon

He looks after Ninotchka, *then makes up his mind and returns down the stairs.*

[**Ground Floor—Eiffel Tower,** *shooting toward the elevator door. The elevator with several passengers is just about to leave when* Leon *hurries into it. The door closes and the elevator starts to ascend quickly.*]

Dissolve to:

Highest Platform—Eiffel Tower

The camera angle *includes the elevator door and a beautiful background view of Paris. The elevator door opens and* Leon *emerges leisurely. He is just about to step to the top of the staircase, when suddenly, to his great amazement, he sees* Ninotchka, *who stands at the balustrade overlooking Paris. She has climbed the tower faster than he despite the elevator. Dumbfounded,* Leon *approaches her.* Ninotchka *turns, very matter-of-fact.*

Ninotchka: You gave me some very valuable information. Thank you.

Leon *(looking at the dazzling view)*: And thank you for getting me up here. I've never seen this before. Beautiful, isn't it?

Ninotchka: Yes, it is.

Leon: I'm glad I saw it before becoming extinct.

Ninotchka: Do not misunderstand me. I do not hold your frivolity against you. *(She looks him up and down)* As basic material you might not be bad, but you are the unfortunate product of a doomed culture. I feel sorry for you.

Leon: You must admit that this doomed old civilization sparkles. . . . It glitters!

Night View of Paris with Its Lights Ablaze, *as seen from the Eiffel Tower.*

33

Ninotchka and Leon

NINOTCHKA: I do not deny its beauty, but it is a waste of electricity. *(See film still 9.)*

LEON: What a city! There are the Grands Boulevards . . . blasted out of the heart of the old streets. The Arc de Triomphe . . . made to greet Napoleon's army. The Opera! And Montmartre . . . Montparnasse . . . La Bohème . . . and now I'll show you the greatest attraction! *(He steps to a telescope and, taking some money from his pocket, drops a coin in the slot)* It will cost me a franc but it is worth it. *(He adjusts the telescope)* The most wonderful spot in all Paris—unique! Here, look. . . . *(She looks in telescope)* What do you see?

NINOTCHKA: I see a house that looks like any other house. What's remarkable about it?

LEON: It's not the structure but the spirit which dwells within. There are three rooms and a kitchenette dedicated to hospitality.

NINOTCHKA: So that is your house?

LEON: Well, let's say I live in it. Such a pleasant place . . . all kinds of comfort, easy to reach, close to street car, bus, and subway. . . .

NINOTCHKA *(straight from the shoulder)*: Does that mean that you want me to go there?

LEON *(feeling that he has offended her)*: Please don't misunderstand me. . . .

NINOTCHKA: Then you don't want me to go there.

LEON *(in a pickle)*: Now I didn't say that either . . . naturally nothing would please me more.

NINOTCHKA *(simply)*: Then why don't we go? *(Looking at him)* You might be an interesting subject of study.

LEON: I will do my best.

They walk toward the elevator as we

Dissolve to:

Interior, Entrance Hall—Leon's Apartment

[*In the foreground stands a console on which is a telephone.*

GASTON, LEON's *elderly, dignified butler, is answering the phone.*

GASTON *(into phone)*: No . . . Count d'Algout is still out. Yes, as soon as he returns I'll tell him. Yes . . . I'll tell him Monsieur Buljanoff.

He puts down the receiver as LEON *opens the door with his key.]* NINOTCHKA *and* LEON *enter.* NINOTCHKA, *during the following scene, is studying every detail of the apartment with the eye of a technical expert.*

LEON: Good evening, Gaston.

GASTON: Good evening, Monsieur.

NINOTCHKA: Is this what you call the "butler"?

LEON: Yes.

NINOTCHKA *(takes* GASTON's *hand)*: Good evening, comrade. *(To* LEON*)* This man is horribly old. You should not make him work.

LEON: He takes good care of that.

NINOTCHKA: He looks sad. Do you whip him?

LEON: No, though the mere thought makes my mouth water.

NINOTCHKA *(to the completely flabbergasted* GASTON*)*: The day will come when you will be free. Go to bed, little father. We want to be alone.

LEON *opens the door to the living room.* NINOTCHKA *enters. Just as he is about to follow her,* GASTON *addresses him.*

GASTON *(in a low voice)*: Count d'Algout, there have been several telephone . . .

LEON: Go to bed.[28]

Interior, Living Room—Leon's Apartment

LEON *enters the room. Closes the door.* NINOTCHKA *is examining the room.*[29]

---

[28] In the film, LEON calls him "little father," too.
[29] In the film, LEON helps her off with her coat and hat and puts them down.

LEON: Well, may I offer you a drink, or how about something to eat?

NINOTCHKA: Thank you. I've had all the calories necessary for today.

LEON *feels a little uncertain as to how to approach this creature.*

NINOTCHKA: What do we do now?

[LEON: We take off our hat and coat. *(He takes her things)* We sit down—we make ourselves comfortable. We adjust ourselves to the prospect of a most enjoyable evening. We look at each other. We smile. *(NINOTCHKA doesn't respond)* Well . . . we don't smile.] How about some music?

NINOTCHKA: Is that customary?

LEON: It helps. It has ever since King David wooed Bathsheba with the harp. As I am not so fortunate as to have my harp at hand, I shall turn on the radio.

[NINOTCHKA *(the observer)*: I should say this room is eighteen by twenty-five.

LEON: Not too big and not too small. What I'd call the typical room of an average man. Or shall we say a little above average.] Now if there are any special aspects you wish to study I have nothing to conceal. Just look around. That's my desk. Those are my books, and here am I. Where shall we begin?

NINOTCHKA: I will start with you.

LEON: That's great. I'm thirty-five years old. Just over six feet tall. I weigh a hundred and eighty-two pounds stripped.

NINOTCHKA: And what is your profession?

LEON: Keeping my body fit, keeping my mind alert, keeping my landlord appeased. That's a full-time job.

NINOTCHKA: And what do you do for mankind?

LEON: For mankind not a thing—for womankind the record is not quite so bleak.

NINOTCHKA: You are something we do not have in Russia.

LEON: Thank you. Thank you.

NINOTCHKA: That is why I believe in the future of my country.

LEON: I begin to believe in it myself since I've met you. I still don't know what to make of it. It confuses me, it frightens me a little, but it fascinates me, Ninotchka.

[NINOTCHKA: You pronounce it incorrectly. Ni-notchka.

LEON: Ni-notchka.

NINOTCHKA: That is correct.]

LEON: Ninotchka, do you like me just a little bit?

NINOTCHKA: Your general appearance is not distasteful.

LEON: Thank you.

NINOTCHKA: Look at me. The whites of your eyes are clear. Your cornea is excellent.

LEON: Your cornea is terrific. Tell me—you're so expert on things —can it be that I'm falling in love with you?

NINOTCHKA: You are bringing in wrong values. Love is a romantic designation for a most ordinary biological, or shall we say chemical, process. A lot of nonsense is talked and written about it.

LEON: Oh, I see. What do you use instead?

NINOTCHKA: I acknowledge the existence of a natural impulse common to all.

LEON: What can I possibly do to encourage such an impulse in you?

NINOTCHKA: You don't have to do a thing. Chemically we are already quite sympathetic.

LEON (bewildered, and yet completely intrigued): You're the most improbable creature I've ever met in my life, Ninotchka, Ninotchka . . .

NINOTCHKA: You repeat yourself.

LEON: I'd like to say it a thousand times.

[NINOTCHKA: Don't do it, please.]

LEON: I'm at a loss, Ninotchka. You must forgive me if I appear a little old-fashioned. After all, I'm just a poor bourgeois.

NINOTCHKA: It's never too late to change. I used to belong to the petty bourgeoisie myself. My father and mother wanted me to stay and work on the farm, but I preferred the bayonet.

LEON *(bewildered)*: The bayonet? Did you really?

NINOTCHKA: I was wounded before Warsaw.

LEON: Wounded? How?

NINOTCHKA: I was a sergeant in the Third Cavalry Brigade. Would you like to see my wound?

LEON *(dumfounded)*: I'd love to. *(She pulls the blouse off her shoulder and shows him her scar)*

LEON: Tsk, tsk, tsk.

NINOTCHKA: A Polish lancer. I was sixteen.

LEON: Poor Ninotchka. Poor, poor Ninotchka.

NINOTCHKA *(readjusting her blouse)*: Don't pity me. Pity the Polish lancer. After all, I'm alive.

> More and more puzzled and fascinated, LEON *sits down close to her.*

LEON: What kind of a girl are you, anyway?

> *(See film strip 10.)*

NINOTCHKA: Just what you see. A tiny cog in the great wheel of evolution.

LEON: You're the most adorable cog I ever saw in my life. Ninotchka, [Cogitska,] let me confess something. Never did I dream I could feel like this toward a sergeant.

> *A clock strikes.*

LEON: Do you hear that?

NINOTCHKA: It's twelve o'clock.

LEON: It's midnight. One half of Paris is making love to the other half. Look at the clock. One hand has met the other hand. They kiss. Isn't that wonderful?

NINOTCHKA: That's the way a clock works. There's nothing wonderful about it. You merely feel you must put yourself in a romantic mood to add to your exhilaration.

LEON: I can't possibly think of a better reason.

NINOTCHKA: It's false sentimentality.

LEON (*trying desperately to make her mood more romantic*): You analyze everything out of existence. You analyze *me* out of existence. I won't let you. Love is not so simple. Ninotchka, Ninotchka, why do doves bill and coo? Why do snails, coldest of all creatures, circle interminably around each other? Why do moths fly hundreds of miles to find their mates? Why do flowers open their petals? Oh, Ninotchka, Ninotchka, surely you feel some slight symptom of the divine passion . . . a general warmth in the palms of your hands . . . a strange heaviness in your limbs . . . a burning of the lips that is not thirst but a thousand times more tantalizing, more exalting, than thirst?

He pauses, waiting for the results of his speech.

NINOTCHKA: You are very talkative.

That is too much for LEON. *He takes her into his arms and kisses her.*

LEON: Was that talkative?

NINOTCHKA: No, that was restful. Again.

Leon kisses her again.

NINOTCHKA: Thank you.

LEON: Oh, my barbaric Ninotchka. My impossible, unromantic, statistical . . .

The telephone rings.

LEON (*continuing*): Glorious, analytical . . .

NINOTCHKA: The telephone is ringing.

LEON: Oh, let it ring.

NINOTCHKA: But one of your friends may be in need of you. You must answer.

LEON *exits out of shot to answer telephone.*

Close Shot—At Desk

LEON *enters, sits down, takes the telephone.*

LEON (*into phone*): Hello? . . . Yes . . . I'm sorry but I couldn't make it. I ran into a friend from the army. . . . What? . . . The deal is off! Are you crazy, Buljanoff? . . .

Close-up—Ninotchka

She is startled by the name.

Leon—at Telephone

LEON: . . . A special envoy arrived. . . . What? . . . That sounds better. I'll be glad to see her any time she wants. . . . Oh, she doesn't want to see me? What do you know about that? Why? . . . Well, I'll get in touch with her myself. What's her name? . . . *(He takes a pencil and a piece of paper)* . . . What? . . . Yaku . . . How do you spell it? . . . Heavens! those Russian names! *(He starts to write it down)* . . . I . . . Oh, Y . . .

> CAMERA PULLS BACK *and* NINOTCHKA *enters the shot. She takes pencil from* LEON's *hand, writes out the name, and leaves again. At first* LEON *is not aware of the full significance of her action. Then it dawns on him.*

LEON *(continuing)*: Yakushova . . . Ninotch . . .

> *At last the situation is entirely clear to him.*

LEON *(into phone)*: All right. Thank you.

> *He hangs up and stares at* NINOTCHKA. *She is putting on her jacket.*

LEON (CAMERA PANNING *with him as he walks over to her)*: Ninotchka . . .

> *He takes her arm.*

NINOTCHKA: I must go.

LEON: Ninotchka, or shall I say Special Envoy Yakushova . . .

NINOTCHKA: Let's forget that we ever met.

LEON: I have a better suggestion. Let's forget that the telephone ever rang. I never heard that you are Yakushova . . . you are Ninotchka . . . my Ninotchka . . .

NINOTCHKA *(firmly)*: I was sent here by my country to fight you.

LEON: All right, fight me, fight me as much as you want, but fight me tomorrow morning! There's nothing sweeter than sharing a secret with a bitter enemy.

40

[NINOTCHKA *(uncompromisingly)*: As a representative of Moscow . . .

LEON: Tonight let's not represent anybody but ourselves.][30]

NINOTCHKA: It is out of the question. If you wish to approach me . . .

LEON: You know I want to . . .

NINOTCHKA: Then do it through my lawyer!

LEON *(desperate)*: Ninotchka, you can't walk out like this . . . I'm crazy about you, and I thought I'd made an impression on you. You liked the white of my eye.

   NINOTCHKA *looks at him for a second, then pulls herself together.*

NINOTCHKA: I must go.

   She starts for the door.

LEON: But, Ninotchka, I held you in my arms. You kissed me! *(See film still 11.)*

NINOTCHKA: I kissed the Polish lancer too . . . before he died.

   As she goes out, we

Fade out

Fade in:

   (NOTE: We have to invent some brief scene to indicate that three days have gone by. From this we)[31]

[30] In the film, instead:
NINOTCHKA: You represent White Russia and I represent Red Russia.
LEON: No, no. Tonight let's not represent anybody but ourselves.
[31] In the film, SWANA is shown in her apartment talking on the telephone: "Yes, Marianne, darling. No, you didn't waken me. I'm not only up—I'm on my way out. Yes, I want to catch Leon, before he rushes out and loses himself in my business affairs. Oh, everything was going perfectly until three days ago—when some horrid female envoy arrived from Moscow. Now we don't know where we are. Yes, I'll telephone you tonight, darling—good-by, dear."

Dissolve to:

The Entrance Hall—Leon's Apartment

The butler opens the door. SWANA *enters, her manner showing her complete familiarity with the place.*

GASTON: Good morning, Your Highness.

SWANA: Good morning, Gaston.

GASTON: Count d'Algout is still asleep.

SWANA *(as she walks toward Leon's room)*: That's all right.

Leon's Bedroom

The curtains are drawn. The night light is still on. LEON, *a dressing gown over his pajamas, is sound asleep in a big arm chair. As* SWANA *enters, she sees him with some alarm.*

SWANA: Leon! What in heaven's name . . . !

LEON: Huh?

SWANA: Is anything wrong? Are you ill?

LEON: No.

SWANA: Don't tell me the bed has lost its best friend.

LEON: I just couldn't sleep. I got up and went back . . . and then got up again. These last few days . . . whew!

SWANA: Darling, you're taking my business affairs far too seriously. Much as I'd love to rob the Bolsheviks of their filthy money, I won't do it at the expense of your health. Particularly as we know we won't get much. *(Tenderly)* You look so pale . . . pale but interesting.

(See film still 12.)

There is a knock at the door.

SWANA: Come in.

GASTON *enters with a breakfast tray.*

GASTON: Your breakfast, monsieur.

LEON: I don't feel like any breakfast.

SWANA: Nonsense. How can you fight the Reds and make yourself agreeable to the Whites if you don't keep up your strength.

GASTON: Shall I draw your bath, sir?

42

LEON: Make it ice cold.

SWANA: Not in your condition. *(To* GASTON*)* Make it tepid, Gaston . . . tepid and tender. And lay out his gray suit. *(To* LEON*)* Afterwards I'll drive you through the Bois. Slowly . . . in Waltz time.

GASTON: A blue shirt, perhaps?

SWANA: Blue? Let's offset his mood. Find a striped one, and brighten it with a great blaze of tie.

GASTON: Very well, Your Highness.

> GASTON *disappears into the bath-dressing room.* SWANA *makes* LEON *sit down and seats herself beside him.*

SWANA: Now . . . here we have two very handsome soft-boiled eggs. Do you suppose hens mind what happens to their eggs? Probably not. They have such unfeeling eyes. We'll put in a great nugget of butter, plenty of pepper and salt. . . . Darling, I haven't seen you for three livelong days . . . seventy-two hours!

LEON *(irritably)*: Oh, please, Swana! I don't know whether I'm standing on my head or my heels. Here you are blaming me for neglecting you when I'm trying to concentrate on another woman and can't get near her.

SWANA: You haven't seen her yet?

LEON: No, and believe me I've tried everything! I must have telephoned her a hundred times. I've sent her telegrams, I've sent her flowers. . . . I asked her to dinner. . . . I offered her seats for the Opera. . . .

SWANA: That proletarian! In the old days we'd have had her flogged.

LEON: That wouldn't have done any good. Not with her. *(Forgetting himself)* She's the most incredible creature I've ever seen.

SWANA: You just told me you hadn't seen her.

LEON: Well . . . er . . . I caught a glimpse of her when she walked through the lobby.

SWANA: Imagine the carpets of a self-respecting Parisian hotel dirtied by the boots of a muzhik! What does she look like?

LEON: You can't imagine.

SWANA: That bad? *(LEON nods)* Old or young?

LEON: Timeless. When she comes into a room you'd think that the Bolsheviks had taken over Paris. She wears her cheap miserable blouse as though it were the latest model by Schiaparelli. What a woman! What a woman! There is a Russian snowstorm in each of her eyes.

SWANA: You saw all that in one glimpse?

LEON *(getting up)*: Darling, if we're going to get anywhere someone has to keep his eyes open! *(He walks over to the bathroom)*

SWANA: Now, darling, soak in your beautiful pine bath and let Gaston shave you.

> LEON *exits into the bathroom. As he does so a bell rings.*

SWANA: Gaston!

> *There is no answer. After a slight pause she herself goes to answer the bell.*

Dissolve to:

Medium Shot—Entrance Hall—Leon's Apartment, *shooting toward the door.*

> SWANA *goes to the door and opens it. The* THREE RUSSIANS *stand outside. Seeing* SWANA, *they are a little intimidated.*

THE THREE RUSSIANS: How do you do?

> SWANA *suspects that for the first time she is being confronted by representatives of the Soviet government.*

SWANA: Yes?

KOPALSKI: We want to talk to Count d'Algout. My name is Kopalski.

SWANA: Oh . . . you are the three gentlemen from Moscow?

KOPALSKI: Yes.

SWANA *(icily)*: You may wait.

> *She closes the door.*

Staircase Hall—in Front of Leon's Door

The THREE RUSSIANS, *very impressed, stand looking at the door which has just been closed.*

BULJANOFF: That's her.

KOPALSKI: Imagine! The niece of the Czar opening the door for us.

BULJANOFF: Once in Petersburg I was driving down the Nevsky Prospect in my cart and Her Highness in her troika swept down from the opposite direction, and when I couldn't make way quick enough she spat in my face.

IRANOFF: Now look here, Buljanoff. You never were in Petersburg, you never owned a cart, and she never spat in your face. Who are you trying to impress?

At this moment the door is opened by LEON *in his bathrobe.*

LEON: Hello, boys.

ALL THREE RUSSIANS: Leon!

LEON: Come in, come in.

They enter.

Living Room—Leon's Apartment

LEON *and the* THREE RUSSIANS *enter.*

LEON: What's new?

KOPALSKI *(excitedly)*: Leon, Leonitchka, she is not going to negotiate! She is going to fight that injunction. She's going to make a precedent of it!

IRANOFF: She says she won't be intimidated by parasites. She called the Duchess a blood-sucking aristocrat and a blackmailer.

LEON *(eagerly)*: What did she say about me?

IRANOFF *(after a moment's consideration)*: I think she covered you with the parasites.

LEON *is disappointed.*

BULJANOFF: And Leonitchka! What she said about *us* . . . !

IRANOFF: And they might believe her in Moscow.

BULJANOFF: What do you mean they might—they *will*!

45

KOPALSKI: We don't blame you, Leon, but when we came from Russia we believed in simplicity. . . .

IRANOFF: We avoided luxury and extravagance and today . . . well, if you were to offer us a glass of champagne, we wouldn't say no.

LEON *is so engrossed in his thoughts that he overlooks the hint.*

LEON: Well, boys, I'd like to help you but what can I do? Yesterday I waited six hours in the lobby!

KOPALSKI: She doesn't leave her room! She has been locked in for the last two days with lawyers and law books!

LEON: All right, then make an appointment with her so I can see her!

KOPALSKI: We can't . . . but you are so ingenious, Leon . . .

IRANOFF: You found your way to us and we weren't easy to reach, were we?

LEON: No, no.

BULJANOFF: Didn't we put up a strong resistance?

LEON: Oh, yes, yes.

KOPALSKI: You must help us, Leon . . . if you don't win her over we're on our way to Siberia!

BULJANOFF: Or it might be the firing squad!

KOPALSKI: Or we can't go back to Russia!

An idea dawns on IRANOFF.

IRANOFF: What's wrong with that?

KOPALSKI *and* BULJANOFF *seize on the same idea.*

BULJANOFF: Yes! We could stay with Leon!

IRANOFF: Leon, how would you like to have three lifelong friends?

LEON: Boys, boys . . . don't forget Russia is your mother country. Three sons walking out all at once . . . that's too much for any mother.

BULJANOFF: Well, if your mother turns against you, you have to look for someone to adopt you.

SWANA's *voice comes from the next room.*

46

SWANA: Leon! Just a minute . . .
LEON *goes back to the other room.*

Leon's Bedroom—Close Shot, *shooting toward the door of the living room.*
SWANA *stands putting on her gloves.*
SWANA: I'm leaving, dear. I'm lunching at Fouquet's if you can make it, and . . . Leon, remember, a man should think it over twice before he decides to become a mother.
She kisses him lightly and walks out.]

Living Room—Royal Suite—Medium Close Shot—at the Desk
It is piled deep with law books and papers. NINOTCHKA *sits at it, conferring with two* LAWYERS.
FIRST LAWYER *(uncertainly)*: I seem to remember some additional injunctive provision dealing with the property of foreigners residing in France.
NINOTCHKA *(with the precision of a machine)*: You are referring to paragraph 59b, section 25f of the Civil Code.
The LAWYERS *exchange a glance of surprise at her knowledge. One of them takes up one of the law books and as he starts to look up the case,* NINOTCHKA *speaks.*
NINOTCHKA: Page eight hundred twenty-four.
Again the LAWYERS *exchange a glance of astonishment.*
NINOTCHKA: And do not fail to read the three footnotes. While you are studying it I will eat. *(She picks up the telephone)* Food please.

A Little Corner in the Room Service Pantry
RAKONIN *is answering the telephone.*
RAKONIN *(into phone)*: Room service. . . . Just a moment please.
He beckons to someone out of the scene. LEON *enters the scene and takes the telephone.*

47

LEON (*with an assumed French accent—into phone*): Room service speaking.

Close Shot—Ninotchka—at the Phone

NINOTCHKA (*into phone*): Send me a plate of raw carrots and beets, beets predominating on a ratio of sixty-forty. . . . What? There is a strike in the kitchen? Good! Will you assure the strikers of my hearty sympathy in their cause. I hope they will not weaken in their demands and tell them to put no dressing whatsoever on my vegetables. . . . What? You won't serve me either? Now look here, Comrade, I think it is a fine idea to let the capitalists go without luncheon but when you keep food away from me you're weakening the people.

Close Shot—Room-Service Pantry—Leon at Phone

LEON (*into phone*): So! You want to make a strike breaker out of me! I am surprised at you, Comrade! Is it too much for the workers of the world to ask you to walk around the corner for lunch? All I can say to you is take your hammer and sickle and get out of that Royal Suite!

He hangs up the telephone with a triumphant smile.

Dissolve to:
Lobby of the Hotel Clarence

NINOTCHKA *emerges from the elevator and starts toward the street. As she passes the showcase of the millinery shop again, she stops and looks at the same hat. Again she shakes her head sadly.*

NINOTCHKA: Tsk, tsk, tsk.

She walks toward the street, as we]

Dissolve to:
Exterior, Hotel Clarence

A taxi is parked at the curb. NINOTCHKA *comes from the hotel and goes to the taxi.*

Close Shot—Ninotchka and Taxi Driver

The DRIVER *puts his hand on the handle of his cab's door expectantly.*

TAXI DRIVER: Where to, madame?

NINOTCHKA: Can you recommend a restaurant?

TAXI DRIVER: Well, there's Pruniers if you care for seafood. If you want to lunch in the Bois, there's . . .

NINOTCHKA *(interrupting)*: Where do you eat?

TAXI DRIVER: At Père Mathieu's.

NINOTCHKA: Where is that?

TAXI DRIVER: It's just a place for workmen.

NINOTCHKA: Where is it?

TAXI DRIVER: Eight blocks down in the Rue de Poivrel.

He opens the door of his cab.

NINOTCHKA: Thank you.

She turns and starts away in the direction he has indicated. The DRIVER *looks after her astounded.*

The CAMERA PANS *from her to the car which stands behind the taxi. It is* LEON's *smart roadster.* LEON *sits at the wheel. He too is looking after* NINOTCHKA, *astonished. He gets out of his car and starts in the direction she has taken. As he does so, we*

Dissolve to:
Paris Street—in Front of Père Mathieu's

Père Mathieu's is a workman's restaurant set a few steps below the level of the sidewalk. A few typical French workmen are going in for lunch. NINOTCHKA *enters the scene, looks around for a second, then goes in too.*

Interior—Père Mathieu's

It is a pleasantly simple place crowded with workmen sitting at lunch. An electric piano is playing. PÈRE MATHIEU, *greeting all his guests like a typical restaurateur, sees* NINOTCHKA *enter.*

PÈRE MATHIEU: This way, madame. Are you alone? By the window perhaps? *(He leads the way)* Or a nice little corner table?

NINOTCHKA: This will do. *(She sits down)*

PÈRE MATHIEU: I think this is the first time you have been to my little place. Your face is new to me. Now, what shall it be?

NINOTCHKA: Raw carrots and beets.

PÈRE MATHIEU *(horrified)*: Oh, madame! This is a restaurant, not a meadow.

He hands her a slate on which the menu is written.

PÈRE MATHIEU: Here is what we are offering today. Please make your choice. I am sure you will find something to tempt your appetite.

Suddenly NINOTCHKA *stares in the direction of the door.*

Medium Shot—at the Door

LEON *has just entered. The* CAMERA *follows him as he makes his way casually in* NINOTCHKA's *direction affecting not to see her. He seats himself at the table directly opposite* NINOTCHKA *and pretends to be overwhelmed with surprise as he sees her.*

LEON: Why, hello! It certainly is a small world!

Shot Including Both Tables

PÈRE MATHIEU *(to* NINOTCHKA*)*: Well, madame? Shall we start with soup? Fish soup today. I got up at five to fish them from the Seine.

LEON *(calling over to* PÈRE MATHIEU*)*: Crayfish soup for me!

Père Mathieu (to Leon): Very well, monsieur. *Back to Ni-notchka)* Then, may I suggest an omelet with mushrooms?
Ninotchka: Bring me something simple. I never think about food.
Père Mathieu *(horrified)*: But, madame! If you don't think about food what do you think about?
Ninotchka: The future of the common people.
Père Mathieu *(sagely)*: That also is a question of food, madame. I'll bring you a nice little lunch *à la* Père Mathieu. *(He exits)*
    Leon *leans toward* Ninotchka *with mock humility.*
Leon: Pardon me for addressing you but you insulted him, you know that. You hurt his feelings. It was just like telling a musician you don't like music. That good old man believes in food as you believe in Karl Marx. You can't go around hurting people, Comrade Yakushova, but maybe you can make it up to him. Do you know how? *(He changes to the chair at his table which is closest to her table)* By eating everything with relish, by drinking everything with gusto, by having a good time for the first time in your natural life!
Ninotchka: I don't like your following me.
Leon: I didn't follow you.
Ninotchka: Then how did you get here?
Leon: I always eat here.
Ninotchka: This is a place for workmen.
Leon *(laying it on thick)*: But my dear child, I am most at home among working men. I hate the places where you circulate—the Hotel Clarence. . . . This is my natural element. After all, what are any of us? Workingmen! At least, those of us who are worth our salt. Hyah?
    He waves off scene to a truckman.

Truckman
    He is in the middle of an enormous gulp of food. He registers surprise, winks at his companion, and then, deciding to humor a drunk, waves back energetically at Leon *in greeting.*

Cut Back to:
Close Shot—Leon and Ninotchka

LEON *has been so successful with the truckman he tries it on another.*

LEON: Hyah!

Another truckman responds with equal exuberance.

Long Shot—Restaurant

LEON, *intoxicated with his success, waves to the whole room.*

LEON: Hyah, fellows!

He gets a wonderful response from all. They realize that a swell drunk is among them.

Leon and Ninotchka

LEON *(boastfully)*: They are all my friends. They're a swell bunch!

PÈRE MATHIEU *enters the shot and serves a plate of soup to* LEON *and one to* NINOTCHKA.

LEON *(trying his bluff on* PÈRE MATHIEU*)*: Ah, my friend! I'm happy to see you again!

PÈRE MATHIEU: I'm always glad to meet a new customer, and I hope this first visit will not be your last.

He exits out of shot.

NINOTCHKA, *her suspicion confirmed, looks at* LEON.

LEON: Just an old man. His memory is getting weak.

NINOTCHKA: What are you after?

LEON: Must one always be after something?

NINOTCHKA: Your tactics are useless. My name is neither Buljanoff, Iranoff, nor Kopalski.

LEON: Oh, Ninotchka, who wants to talk business. If *you* win the suit, fine. If *we* win the suit, better. You do me an injustice. *(He moves over to her table, leaving the soup at his table)* When we went to my apartment did I have the slightest idea that you had any connection with this deal?

52

NINOTCHKA: But you have now, and I know now that you are a man who employs business methods which in Russia would be punished by death.

LEON: Death! Death! Always so glum! What about life, Ninotchka! Do Russians never think of life? Of the moment in which we are living? The only moment we really have? Don't take it all so seriously, Ninotchka. Nothing is worth it. Please . . . relax . . . I beg you, Sergeant . . . smile!

NINOTCHKA *(astonished)*: What?

LEON: Will you smile?

NINOTCHKA: Why?

LEON: Just smile.

NINOTCHKA: At what?

LEON: At anything. At the whole ludicrous spectacle of life. At people being pompous and taking themselves seriously and exaggerating their own importance. If you can't find anything else to laugh at you can laugh at you and me.

NINOTCHKA: Why?

LEON: Because we are an odd couple.

NINOTCHKA: Then you should go back to your table.

LEON: No, I can't leave you. I won't. Not yet. Not until I've made you laugh . . . at least once.

> *To get rid of him* NINOTCHKA *emits a joyless sound which approximates a laugh.*

NINOTCHKA: Ha! Ha! Now go back.

LEON: That's not a laugh! I mean a laugh from the heart. Now let's see. I'm going to tell you a funny story. Just a moment . . . I've got it! Well, it seems there were a couple of Frenchmen who went to America . . .

NINOTCHKA: On which boat?

LEON *(thrown off by her methodical thinking)*: Well, er . . . let's drop it. I don't think you would care for that one.

NINOTCHKA: Probably not.

LEON: Do you like Scotch stories?

53

NINOTCHKA: I have never heard one.

LEON: Two Scotchmen met on the street . . . and I don't know the name of the street and it really doesn't matter. Well, anyway, one's name was McIntosh and the other's was McGillicuddy. McIntosh says to McGillicuddy, "Hello, Mr. McGillicuddy," and McGillicuddy says to McIntosh, "Hello, Mr. McIntosh," and then McIntosh says to McGillicuddy, "How is Mrs. McGillicuddy?" and then McGillicuddy says to McIntosh, "How is Mrs. McIntosh?" . . .

NINOTCHKA: I wish they had never met.

LEON *(disarmed)*: So do I. *(After a little pause)* Now, here's a great one. . . . Ha! Ha! Ha! *(He looks at* NINOTCHKA *and her expression stops him)* Well, maybe it's not so good. Let's forget it! How's this? Two men are looking at the moon. One says to the other, "Is it true that a lot of people live on the moon?" "Yes, it is," says the other, "five hundred million." "Whew!" replies the first, "they must get pretty crowded when it's half moon!" Ha! Ha! Ha!

There is no response from NINOTCHKA.

LEON *(starting to get sore)*: I suppose you don't think that's funny?

NINOTCHKA: No.

LEON: It seemed funny to me when I first heard it. Maybe the trouble isn't with the joke. Maybe it's with you!

NINOTCHKA: I don't think so.

LEON: Maybe you haven't any sense of humor. Well, I'll give you one more chance! Now listen!

He gets up and speaks in a threatening voice audible to the entire room.

LEON: When I heard this joke for the first time I laughed myself sick. Here goes! A man comes into a restaurant and sits down and says, "Waiter! Get me a cup of coffee without cream." After five minutes the waiter comes back and says, "I'm sorry, sir, we're all out of cream, can it be without milk?"

1

2

3

4

6

7

8

9

10

11

12

13

14

15

16

17

18

19

20

21

22

23

24

25

26

A Group of Several Workmen

They have overheard the story and all burst into laughter.

Ninotchka and Leon

NINOTCHKA *continues to eat her soup without a shadow of a laugh.*

LEON *(furious)*: Not funny, huh?

NINOTCHKA: No.

LEON: So you don't think that's funny? It *is* funny! Everyone else thinks so! Maybe you didn't get it.

He sits down again.

LEON *(threateningly)*: I'll tell you that joke again. A man comes into a restaurant. Did you get that?

NINOTCHKA: Yes.

LEON: He sits down at the table and says to the waiter. . . . Did you get that too?

NINOTCHKA: Yes.

LEON: Well, so far it isn't funny, but wait. He says to the waiter, "Waiter! Bring me a cup of coffee." So the waiter comes back five minutes later and says, "I'm sorry, sir, we have no coffee." . . . *(He realizes he has made a mistake)* Wait a minute . . . wait a minute . . . I'm all mixed up. . . . *(He starts over again)* A man comes in a restaurant, he sits down, he calls the waiter and he says, "Waiter! Get me a cup of coffee without cream," and five minutes later the waiter comes back and says, "I'm sorry, sir, we have no cream, can it be a glass of milk!"

He gets up and goes over to his table furiously.

LEON: Ah! You have no sense of humor! That settles it! You have no sense of humor! *None*! No humor!!

In his excitement he leans on the shaky table. It topples forward. Simultaneously his feet shoot from under him and he sits violently on the floor, the contents of the table crashing about him, hot soup in his face.

A terrific roar of laughter arises; the whole restaurant is rocking with laughter.

For a split second NINOTCHKA *makes an effort to control the irresistible impulse to laugh but loses the battle and herself roars with laughter.*

LEON *(indignantly)*: What's funny about this?

NINOTCHKA'S *laughter is uncontrollable.*

After a moment LEON *gets up and sits next to her. As he dries himself with his napkin he sees the humor of the situation and starts to howl with laughter too. The ice is broken at last!*

On their mutual wild hilarity, we

Fade out

Fade in:

Living Room—Royal Suite

*A conference is in session—*NINOTCHKA, *her two* LAWYERS, *and the* THREE RUSSIANS. NINOTCHKA *sits at the desk, leaning back in the chair, looking into space, and apparently weighing every point which is brought up. One of the lawyers is reading from a document.*

(See film still 13.)

LAWYER *(reading)*: In addition to the arguments above enumerated for lifting this injunction, we wish to cite the decision of the High Court of Paris, rendered in the case of Princess Marishka against the Government of Montenegro on the fifth day of August, 1897. Comparing the facts in that case with our present set of facts we feel that the Treaty between the Republic of France and the U.S.S.R. should prevail over all. . . .

Suddenly NINOTCHKA *laughs. Everyone looks at her astonished.* NINOTCHKA *gets up.*

NINOTCHKA: I'm sorry, gentlemen. The other day I heard such a funny story. . . . (She laughs again) It still makes me laugh. It is very funny. (A little embarrassed) I am sorry. Oh yes . . . about this injunction . . .

LAWYER (very businesslike): The hearing is set for the twentieth of this month.

NINOTCHKA (not thinking of the injunction): That's two weeks from Thursday . . .

LAWYER: We did our utmost to have it set ahead.

NINOTCHKA her attitude completely different from her former business conferences): I know, gentlemen, but it is in the hands of the Court. We're helpless, aren't we?

LAWYER: Yes. It is unfortunate.

NINOTCHKA: Well, there's nothing we can do about it. Why get excited?

> The THREE RUSSIANS as well as the LAWYERS are puzzled.
> The RUSSIANS exchange hopeful glances.

LAWYER: We'll leave these papers here for your further consideration. Au revoir, madame.

NINOTCHKA: Au revoir.

> The LAWYERS leave.

> Left alone with the RUSSIANS, NINOTCHKA is unable to conceal her happiness entirely.

NINOTCHKA: Well, it means another two weeks in Paris.

IRANOFF (with exaggerated efficiency): Too bad we have to waste all that time.

KOPALSKI: I acted on your suggestion and got in touch with the Power and Light authorities. Whenever you want to visit their plants they are open to you.

NINOTCHKA (a little bit dreamily): Oh yes, Power and Light. Thank you.

BULJANOFF: There's something else which I know will appeal to you. A visit to the Paris sewers. They tell me it is extremely instructive.

NINOTCHKA: Huh? . . . Why don't you get a haircut, Buljanoff?

You all look so wintry, Comrades. And why do we always keep the windows closed? *(She opens the window)* Isn't it amazing, at home there's still snow and ice and here . . . Look at the birds. I always felt a little hurt that our swallows deserted us in the winter for capitalistic countries. Now I know why. We have the high ideal but they have the climate . . . well, Comrades, I don't think I need you any more.

KOPALSKI:[32] If there is anything we can do for you . . .

NINOTCHKA: No, not a thing. Would you like to go out?

ALL THREE RUSSIANS: Thank you, Comrade.

NINOTCHKA: Have you any money?

> *The* RUSSIANS *stammer a negative answer.*
>
> *Smiling benevolently,* NINOTCHKA *goes to the table, takes several bills from her handbag, and goes back, extending a fifty-franc bill to* KOPALSKI.

NINOTCHKA: Well, here are fifty francs.

ALL THREE RUSSIANS *(overwhelmed)*: Thank you, Comrade, thank you.

NINOTCHKA: Bring me forty-five back.

ALL THREE RUSSIANS *(terribly disappointed)*: Naturally, Comrade.

> *The* THREE RUSSIANS *leave. Ninotchka waits a moment. Then hurries to the door and turns the key.* CAMERA FOLLOWS HER *as she goes into the bedroom. She proceeds to the door leading to the corridor and turns its key. She goes to the table and takes a little key from her handbag, goes to the bureau and unlocks the drawer, opens it, and, just as she is about to take out something, her eye falls on the night table, where she sees the picture of Lenin which she brought with her from Moscow. She walks over to it and turns its face against the wall, then goes back to the bureau and takes from the drawer the very hat which twice aroused her disapproval when it was displayed in the millinery shop in the lobby.*

---

[32] In the film, IRANOFF speaks this line.

She moves over to the large mirror, puts the hat on her head, is uncertain whether it is right side to fore, and changes it. She looks at herself, aghast at seeing a complete stranger. She sits down, still staring in the mirror, then leans forward and rests her chin on her hand. As she sits studying the new Ninotchka suspiciously, we

Dissolve to:
Living Room—Leon's Apartment
> *It is evening.* LEON *is walking nervously up and down.* GASTON *is puttering over the drink table.*

LEON *(consulting his watch)*: What time have you, Gaston?

GASTON: Eight forty-two, sir.

LEON: I guess it is eight forty-two.

GASTON: You seem to be a bit nervous, sir.

LEON: I am, Gaston.

GASTON: If you will forgive me, ever since you met that Bolshevik lady I've noticed a distinct change in you, sir.

LEON *(complacently)*: Have you?

GASTON: Decidedly. Yesterday I was greatly amazed when I came from the market and found that you had made your bed, sir.

LEON: And Gaston, I was happier all day long. I felt I'd contributed something.

[GASTON: Well, sir, if you should do it again, which I hope you won't, please remember the order. Counterpane, blanket, blanket, sheet, sheet.

LEON: Ah, there's something poetic about the simple processes of labor. Counterpane, blanket, blanket, sheet, sheet . . . it should be set to music!]

GASTON: May I add, sir, that it was with great amazement that I found a copy of Karl Marx's *Capital* on your night table. That is a socialistic volume which I refuse to so much as dust, sir. I view with alarm, sir, the influence over you of this Bolshevik lady.

LEON: I can't follow you, Gaston, isn't it about time that you realized the unfairness of your position? You being my servant? Wouldn't you like to stand on an equal footing with me?

GASTON: No, sir.

LEON: Isn't there any revolt in you? Sometimes when I order you around don't you feel like kicking me in the pants?

GASTON (*emphatically*): No, sir.

LEON: Oh, you're a reactionary! Don't you look forward to the day when you can come in here and stand square on your two feet and say, "Hey, you, d'Algout! from now on it's going to be share and share alike"?

GASTON (*outraged*): Emphatically not, sir. The prospect terrifies me. Now, don't misunderstand me, sir, I don't resent your not paying me for the past two months, but the thought that I should split my bank account with you . . . that you should take half of my life's savings . . . that is really too much for me.

The door bell rings. GASTON *starts for the door. With a gesture* LEON *stops him.*

LEON: Go to bed, little father, go to bed.

GASTON *leaves through the other door as* LEON *exits toward the entrance hall.*

Entrance Hall—Leon's Apartment

LEON *enters the scene. He opens the door. Outside stands* NINOTCHKA *wearing her new hat timidly as well as a completely new outfit which she has bought, apparently to match the new hat. It takes* LEON *a few seconds to digest her new splendor. He takes her hand and leads her in, closing the door. He looks at her again and kisses her hand.*

(See film still 14.)

NINOTCHKA: I don't look too foolish?

LEON: Foolish? If this dress were to walk down the boulevard all by itself I would follow it from one end of Paris to the other, and when I caught up with it I would say, "Just a moment, you charming little dress, I want you to meet Ninotchka . . . you two were meant for each other."

NINOTCHKA *feels more comfortable.*

LEON *leads her into the living room.*

Living Room—Leon's Apartment

They both enter. NINOTCHKA *pauses a second and looks around.*

LEON: You remember this room?

NINOTCHKA: I've never been here before. I wonder whom you're thinking of. Oh, I know, a girl with a map, figuring out each step, worrying about north and south. Today . . . now this might shock you . . . I went up to a taxi and said "Eight Rue du Bois" . . . and here I am.

LEON: You see? Life can be so simple.

NINOTCHKA: For twelve francs, seventy-five.

LEON: Twelve seventy-five from the Clarence? The son-of-a-gun made a detour! . . . *(Charmingly)* But he got you here.

At this moment the clock starts to strike. They both look toward it.

Insert—Clock

The hands register nine o'clock.

Leon and Ninotchka

LEON *wants to take her in his arms. She resists a little.*

NINOTCHKA *(reprimanding him)*: It's nine o'clock.

LEON: That's when one half of Paris says to the other half, "What are your plans for this evening, madame?"

NINOTCHKA *(getting more and more in the spirit of her change of appearance)*: Well, first I should like to take off my hat [and jacket]. (LEON *takes them)* Then could we have some music?

LEON: A wonderful idea! Radio or records?

NINOTCHKA: Not radio. Let's have music that's just for ourselves.

LEON *turns on the victrola.*

LEON *(with great feeling and sincerity)*: I'll play it softly because I have things to tell you about which I can't shout.

He walks back to NINOTCHKA, *who by now is seated in an armchair. He sits on the arm of the chair. He tries to make a declaration of his love. He stammers several words.*

LEON: Well, my darling . . . I . . . we . . .

It is no use. In a sudden outburst of emotion he takes her in his arms and kisses her.

LEON *(as they come out of the kiss)*: You see I couldn't shout that.

NINOTCHKA *(with great feeling)*: Leon, you know the jokes you told me a few days ago? I wake up in the middle of the night and laugh at them. Now, Leon that's wrong. I know they're not funny, they're silly. They're stupid. And still . . . I laugh. . . . and when I look at Buljanoff and Iranoff and Kopalski I know they are scoundrels and I should hate them—then I realize who made them like that, and instead of sending my report to Moscow I tear it up and go down and buy a ridiculous hat . . . and if this keeps on . . . am I too talkative?

(See film still 15.)

LEON *(radiantly)*: No . . . go on.

NINOTCHKA: Leon, I want to tell you something which I thought I never would say, which I thought nobody ever should say, because I thought it didn't exist . . . and, Leon . . . I can't say it . . .

They kiss again. As the kiss ends they look at each other for a second.

NINOTCHKA *gets up and goes toward the desk, sits in the desk chair, opens her handbag, which lies there, and takes from it a little mirror and a lipstick. Before she uses it she looks at* LEON *with guilty happiness.* LEON *looks at her with great tenderness and walks over to the desk and stands looking at her as she makes up her lips.*

LEON: What a gesture for a sergeant.

As soon as she is finished, NINOTCHKA *slips the mirror and lipstick back into her handbag and, as she does so, glances at the top of the desk.*

NINOTCHKA: Leon, I would like to ask you something.

LEON: Anything, Ninotchka.

NINOTCHKA: If you don't want to answer, you needn't. But if you do, you must tell me the truth.

LEON: I promise . . . I swear.

NINOTCHKA *(seriously)*: Did you make any change in this room?

LEON: I don't think so.

NINOTCHKA: When I was here before I noticed a photograph of a woman on the desk in a wide silver frame. I thought what a waste of silver. That's all that interested me then. Now I would like to know . . . what happened to the woman?

LEON too is completely serious by now. For answer he quietly opens the drawer of the desk. NINOTCHKA *looks in and takes from the drawer the photograph. As she looks at it she rises.*

NINOTCHKA: The Duchess.

LEON *nods gravely.*

NINOTCHKA *(looking at the picture)*: She is very attractive. She has great elegance. *(She looks back at* LEON*)* She's what you call a woman of the world, isn't she?

LEON *(after a little pause)*: Ninotchka, I love you.

NINOTCHKA: I suppose she is very entertaining. . . . It must be lots of fun to be with her, so witty, so glamorous. . . .

LEON: Ninotchka, you're jealous.

NINOTCHKA *nods sadly.*

NINOTCHKA *(with great feeling)*: Leon, don't ever ask me for a picture of myself . . . I couldn't bear the thought of being shut up in a drawer . . . I couldn't breathe, I couldn't stand it.

LEON: My darling.

As he takes her in his arms, we

Fade out

Fade in:

Interior, Smart Night Club

DUCHESS SWANA *enters with a party consisting of* GENERAL SAVITZKY *and five other smartly dressed people of the world. The* HEADWAITER *hurries to greet* SWANA.

HEADWAITER: Good evening, Your Highness.

SWANA: Good evening, Louis. You seem to be very crowded tonight. Can you manage a table near the floor?

HEADWAITER: Certainly, Your Highness, this way please. . . . Count d'Algout made the reservation this afternoon.

SWANA *(puzzled)*: Count d'Algout . . .

HEADWAITER: It is only a small table but it will be no trouble to put in some extra chairs.

SWANA *has grasped the situation by now.*

SWANA: No, that's another party.

In order to save the situation one of the ladies makes a suggestion.

LADY: Why don't we go some other place? It's so crowded here.

SWANA *(delighted at her luck)*: No, no! This is glory! At last I'm going to have a look at that female Bolshevik. Can you give us another table?

HEADWAITER: Only one in the rear, I'm afraid.

SWANA: That's perfect!

CAMERA MOVES *with the group as the* HEADWAITER *leads it toward a table.*

64

ANOTHER WOMAN GUEST: You mean Leon's bringing the Bolshevik you told us about?

SWANA: Isn't it divine?

ANOTHER GUEST: I wouldn't have missed this for the world.

SWANA *(very gay, in anticipation of a triumph)*: Now, we must be very discreet. If she sucks her soup and drinks out of her finger bowl, I don't want anyone to laugh. *(Everybody in the party giggles)* We must not embarrass little Leon. He is going through enough for my sake. We mustn't add insult to injury

By now they have reached the table in the rear.

HEADWAITER: Is this satisfactory?

SWANA: Thank you, Louis.

They sit down. The HEADWAITER *bends over* GENERAL SAVITZKY, *an elderly Russian aristocrat, who sits next to* SWANA.

HEADWAITER: Is it to be dinner, monsieur?

GENERAL SAVITZKY: Possibly later. We'll just start with champagne.

SWANA *(to the party)*: I'm only afraid that the doorman may spoil our fun. If only he lets her in!

SWANA *laughs and everyone joins in her laughter.*

[GENERAL SAVITZKY: Your Highness . . .

SWANA: Yes, General Savitzky?

GENERAL SAVITZKY: I want you to know all the White Russian exiles in Paris are keeping their fingers crossed about the jewels. They are very interested in the case.

SWANA *suspects her countrymen.*

SWANA: Are they indeed? Thank you.

GENERAL SAVITZKY: They hope the settlement will bring you a fortune.

SWANA: General, please . . . if you hear any rumors that I am a charitable person, will you please kill them at their source?

As she is lighting a cigarette a guest suddenly looks toward the entrance and sees LEON.]

GUEST: Look! There's Leon!

Joyfully SWANA *looks toward the entrance, as does everyone else at the table.*
EVERYONE AT THE TABLE: Oh yes! Where? There! Oh! How exciting!

Close Shot—Leon at the Entrance
Suddenly, through the door of the cloakroom comes NI-NOTCHKA, radiant in a beautiful evening gown.

Swana's Table
SWANA's *expression freezes as she sees* NINOTCHKA. *The rest of the guests stare in an embarrassed silence, save for one bird-brained little guest, named* MARIANNE, *who feels it her mission to save the situation.*
MARIANNE: Isn't she something?
A neighbor nudges her warningly. SWANA *withers her with a glance and rises.*
SWANA: Shall we dance, General Savitzky?
SWANA *and the General leave for the dance floor.* [*The guest who has nudged her turns to* MARIANNE.
GUEST: Are you crazy?
ANOTHER GUEST: How could you make such a remark?
THIRD GUEST: Swana isn't stupid.
MARIANNE: What did I say? I just said "isn't she something?" I didn't say something what.]

Close Shot—Leon's Table
LEON *and* NINOTCHKA *are seated and a* WAITER *stands by them presenting a bottle of champagne to* LEON *for his approval.*
LEON (*to* WAITER): Is it dry?
WAITER: Yes, monsieur.
LEON (*to* NINOTCHKA): Is that right or do you prefer it sweet?

NINOTCHKA: I wouldn't know. The closest I ever came to champagne was in a newsreel. The wife of some president was throwing it at a battleship.

LEON: It's always good luck to launch something with champagne; a battleship . . . or an evening.

By now the WAITER *is filling their glasses.* NINOTCHKA *lifts her glass and looks at it.*

NINOTCHKA: It's funny to look back. I was brought up on goat's milk, I had a ration of vodka in the army, and now champagne.

LEON *(gaily)*: From goats to grapes. That's drinking in the right direction.

NINOTCHKA *takes her first sip of champagne.* LEON *drinks and watches her. The first sip proves a painful surprise.* NINOTCHKA's *face is that of a child who has been fed a bad medicine.*

NINOTCHKA: Ugh . . . um . . . oh . . . *(Slowly the delight of champagne dawns on her and her face breaks into a smile)* It's good.

She drinks the whole glass at once. LEON *looks at her in amused surprise. He drinks too. The* WAITER *fills their glasses again.*

NINOTCHKA: From what I read I thought champagne was a strong drink. It's very delicate. Do people ever get drunk on this?

LEON: There have been cases . . . but the headache the next morning is worth while—if you drink it with the right toast. *(He raises his glass again fondly)* To us, Ninotchka!

They clink glasses and drink again, looking at each other.

Long Shot of the Table, *including part of the dance floor. As* LEON *and* NINOTCHKA *lift their glasses again,* SWANA *and* GENERAL SAVITZKY *start to dance by the table.* SWANA *stops, pretending complete astonishment.*

SWANA: Hello, Leon! What a surprise! You of all people! How are you, my dear?

LEON *gets up.* NINOTCHKA *watches the scene tensely.*

LEON *(embarrassed)*: Hello, Swana. How do you do, General Savitzky?

GENERAL SAVITZKY: How do you do?

SWANA *(to* LEON*)*: You're looking magnificent, Leon . . . *(To* GENERAL SAVITZKY*)* . . . isn't he, General Savitzky?

GENERAL SAVITZKY: Yes.

> LEON *knows that* SWANA *wants to embarrass him but is embarrassed nevertheless.*

LEON: Thank you.

SWANA: Is this your new dress suit?

LEON: Yes, Swana.

SWANA: Didn't I tell you Benson and Benson were the tailors for you?

LEON *(patiently)*: Yes, Swana, you did.

SWANA: It's a dream of beauty. He never takes my word for anything, but I was right, wasn't I?

LEON: Yes, Swana.

SWANA *(forcing an introduction)*: Am I interrupting?

LEON: Not at all. Your Highness, may I present Madame Yakushova?[33]

SWANA: How do you do?

NINOTCHKA: How do you do?

LEON: And General Savitzky.

GENERAL SAVITZKY: How do you do?

NINOTCHKA: How do you do?

SWANA: I've some wonderful news for you, Leon. It's about Punchy . . . do you mind if I sit down?

LEON *(realizing that he cannot prevent it)*: No . . . please . . .
> SWANA *sits down.*

SWANA *(to* GENERAL SAVITZKY*)*: General, would you mind making my excuses at our table? I'll be back in a few moments.

---

[33] In the film, instead, LEON introduces her as Comrade Yakushova.

GENERAL SAVITZKY: Certainly.

He bows and leaves.

Close Shot—All Three Sitting at the Table

SWANA: Well, Leon, we can be proud of our Punchy. He had a triumph at the dog show.

During the following speech, NINOTCHKA's expression does not change. She knows exactly the game SWANA is playing.

SWANA *(continuing)*: He won another blue ribbon and bit the judge. Ha! ha! ha! I bought him the cutest sweater as a reward. You should see him strut down the street in it. He looks like a little boulevardier. *(To NINOTCHKA)* You see, Count d'Algout gave me Punchy for my birthday. *(To LEON)* You must have searched weeks before you found anything as divine as Punchy, didn't you, Leon?

LEON *(fed up with SWANA's tactics)*: Months, Swana.

SWANA *(to NINOTCHKA)*: Poor Madame Yakushova . . . here we are talking in mysteries. . . . I'm sure you wonder what it's all about.

NINOTCHKA *(dry and direct)*: Not at all. . . . I understand perfectly, Count d'Algout gave you a dog. You made it very clear, madame.

SWANA: Dear me . . . I must be losing my finesse. If I'm not careful I'll be understood by everybody.

LEON *(acutely uncomfortable)*: There's a charming crowd here tonight, isn't there?

SWANA: I'm going, Leon . . . *(She rises, as does LEON, delighted to get rid of her)* but before I leave I must compliment you on your gown, Madame Yakushova. Is that what they're wearing in Moscow this year?

NINOTCHKA: No, last year, madame.

SWANA *sits again, as does* LEON.

SWANA: Isn't it amazing! One gets a wrong impression of the new

Russia. *(Cynically)* It must be charming. I'm glad conditions are so improved. I assume this is what the factory workers wear at their dances?

NINOTCHKA: Exactly. You see, it would have been embarrassing for people of my sort to wear low-cut gowns in the old Russia. The lashes of the Cossacks across our backs were not very becoming, and you know how vain women are.

SWANA: You're absolutely right about the Cossacks. We made an unpardonable mistake when we let them use their [knouts].[34] They had such reliable guns.

> LEON *has grown more and more uncomfortable as the two ladies fence.*

LEON: Will you do me a favor? Stop talking about the good old days.

SWANA: A very wise suggestion, Leon. I'm afraid madame and I will never agree. *(She plays her trump card)* The only thing we have in common is our lawsuit and that will be decided next week. I understand everything will be over by Thursday. Am I right?

> NINOTCHKA *and* LEON *realize the malice and yet the truth of her words.*

NINOTCHKA: You're right, madame, it will all be over by Thursday.

SWANA *(rubbing it in)*: It is unfortunate that you have so few more days in Paris. *(She turns to* LEON*)* Be sure and redouble your efforts so that madame can take some pleasant memories when she returns to Moscow. *(She rises,* LEON *rising too) Good night. (*NINOTCHKA *nods without answering. To* LEON*)* Good night, Leon.

LEON *(coldly)*: Good night, Swana.

> SWANA *leaves the table.* LEON *sits again. The mood of the two has been changed by the problem of their separation, which has been brought before them. They sit in silence for a moment.* NINOTCHKA *speaks first.*

NINOTCHKA: Now I think I need a glass of champagne.

---

[34] In the film she says "whips."

LEON *fills their glasses. They drink. Then* LEON *takes* NI-NOTCHKA's *hand.*

NINOTCHKA *(trying to break the mood)*: Quickly, please . . . tell me one of your funny stories.

LEON: A funny story?

NINOTCHKA: You never finished the one about the two Scotchmen with the names.

LEON: Well, there were two Scotchmen. One was named McIntosh and one was named McGillicuddy. They met on the street.

He stops.

NINOTCHKA: Go on.

LEON: No, darling. I'll tell you another story, a much better one. *(With deep sincerity)* The only thing that will be over on Thursday is the lawsuit. There will be no Thursday for us. Not next week or any week. We won't let it happen. I'll tear it out of the calendar. Is that a good story?

NINOTCHKA *(touched)*: Wonderful—if one could believe it.

LEON: You must, darling.

NINOTCHKA *(lifting her glass)*: To the loveliest story I ever heard.

They drink. The orchestra starts a number.

NINOTCHKA *(afraid of where the conversation may lead)*: Shall we dance?

They both start toward the dance floor.

Close Shot—Leon and Ninotchka, *dancing a waltz. At the second turn* NINOTCHKA *starts to feel the effect of the champagne.*

NINOTCHKA *(tipsily)*: Oo! Darling! Something is the matter.

LEON: You just made that trip from goats to grapes a little too fast.

NINOTCHKA: Oh, everything is so wonderful! It's getting farther and farther away!

LEON: What, darling?

NINOTCHKA: Thursday.

LEON: Yes. Don't worry. Everything will be all right.

In the gayest mood, NINOTCHKA *addresses the crowd on the dance floor.*

NINOTCHKA: Comrades! Comrades!

LEON *(embarrassed)*: Darling, darling . . . please!

NINOTCHKA: I must talk to my brothers!

LEON: Shhh! Shhh!

NINOTCHKA: Don't shush me. I am People! I want to make a speech. I want to overthrow the Duchess!

LEON *starts to lead her off the dance floor.*

LEON: But, darling, you can't do that.

NINOTCHKA: Comrades! Good people of France!

LEON: Now, Ninotchka . . . please!

NINOTCHKA: They are all Duchesses here . . . thousands of Duchesses . . . and I am going to tell them.

By now they have almost reached the powder room.

LEON: Quite right . . . yes, yes, yes, but first you're going in that door and you're going to take a little spirits of ammonia and lie down.

NINOTCHKA *(sweetly)*: No speech?

LEON *(as though he were addressing a little child)*: No speech.

NINOTCHKA: I love you, my little Leonitchka!

LEON: And I adore you, NINOTCHUA.[35]

NINOTCHKA *goes unsteadily into the powder room.* LEON *wipes his forehead in relief and goes to the bar, followed by the* CAMERA.

LEON *(to the bartender)*: Give me a double brandy.

Close Shot—Door of the Powder Room

A group of four to six women come out whispering excitedly about something which must have happened within.

---

[35] In the film, LEON continues, "Go ahead, now."
NINOTCHKA: No speech?
LEON: No! No! For heaven's sake, no speech!
NINOTCHKA: No speech.

CAMERA *goes with them as they go to the* MANAGER *of the restaurant and crowd about him and whisper what has happened.*

Close Shot—Bar

The bartender gives LEON *his double brandy and* LEON *tosses it off. The* MANAGER *comes into the shot and addresses* LEON.

MANAGER *(very excitedly)*: I'm very sorry, Count d'Algout, it is most embarrassing, but the lady you brought with you tonight is spreading communistic propaganda in the powder room.

LEON *stares at him for a second, then turns to the bartender.*

LEON: Give me another double brandy.

MANAGER: That kind of propaganda is bad anywhere, but inciting the attendants of a powder room to go on strike. . . . Well, if she succeeds the consequences will be disastrous.

LEON: What can I do about it?

MANAGER: She has been asked to leave the powder room but without success. We would appreciate if you would see to it yourself.

LEON *(horrified)*: You want me to go in there?

MANAGER: I'm sorry, sir, but I must insist.

The MANAGER *bows and walks away.* LEON *gulps down the second double brandy. The* CAMERA *follows him as he proceeds toward the powder room like a hero going into battle. Just as he is about to enter, a very dignified elderly lady comes out, is surprised at his attempted entrance, and glares at him.* LEON *loses his courage and* FOLLOWED BY THE CAMERA *goes back to the bar to strengthen it with some of the Dutch variety.*

LEON *(completely exhausted—to the bartender)*: Make it a triple brandy. *As we*

Dissolve to:
Living Room—the Royal Suite

RAKONIN, *the waiter, opens the door.* NINOTCHKA *and* LEON, *both very tipsy by now, enter the room.* LEON *is carrying a*

73

bottle of champagne in a napkin. As he passes the waiter he speaks:

LEON *(to* RAKONIN*)*: All right . . . you can tell the Duchess . . . you can tell everybody . . . they know anyhow . . . it doesn't make any difference . . . now get out!

RAKONIN, *who seems very interested in the situation, closes the door.*

LEON *goes to* NINOTCHKA. *Both sit on a couch.*

NINOTCHKA *(moving close to him)*: Don't tell them where we're going, sweetheart.

LEON: No. Nobody will find us.

NINOTCHKA *is lyrically tight. Through her there shines a great happiness.*

NINOTCHKA: Are we going to build our little house?

LEON: Yes . . . a little white house.

NINOTCHKA: Not white, darling.

LEON: All right, we'll make it red.

(See film still 16.)

NINOTCHKA: No, don't let's have it any color . . . no color . . . just a house house . . . let's form our own party.

LEON: Right: Lovers of the world unite!

NINOTCHKA *(delighted)*: And we won't stretch up our arms . . .

LEON: No! No!

NINOTCHKA: . . . and we won't clench our fist . . .

LEON: No! No!

NINOTCHKA *(tenderly)*: Our salute will be a kiss.

LEON: Yes . . . a kiss . . . salute!

She sinks into his arms and they kiss.

NINOTCHKA *(still in his arms)*: I am so happy. No one can be so happy without being punished. I will be punished and I should be punished. *(She gets up)* I want to confess, darling.

LEON: I know . . . it's the Russian soul.

NINOTCHKA *(her gaiety mixed with sadness)*: Everyone wants to confess and if they don't confess they make them confess. I am a traitor. When I kissed you I betrayed the Russian ideal. Leon, I should be stood up against the wall.

LEON *gets up.*

LEON *(sympathetically)*: Would that make you any happier?

NINOTCHKA: Much happier.

LEON: All right.

Still carrying the champagne bottle, LEON leads her to the end of the room and stands her against the wall. He takes the napkin from the champagne bottle and puts it over her eyes. The CAMERA moves with him as he goes away from NINOTCHKA, and as he walks he starts to open the champagne. The cork pops.

Close Shot—Ninotchka, *as she sinks gently into a chair.*

NINOTCHKA *(happily)*: I have paid the penalty. Now let's have some music.

Close Shot—Ninotchka and Leon

LEON: Let's turn on the radio.

NINOTCHKA: Radio! What is radio?

LEON: It's a little box that you buy on the installment plan and before you tune it in they tell you they have a new model.

NINOTCHKA *(getting up)*: Oh yes, yes. It has a little knob that turns . . . a little knob . . . it must be somewhere around here . . . yes . . . here . . . I see . . .

Confusedly NINOTCHKA starts looking for something, repeating, "a little knob . . . a little knob." Followed by LEON she goes toward the safe, opens the concealing door, and both are delighted as they see the safe's dial.

NINOTCHKA *(triumphantly)*: Here it is!

LEON *nods approval and starts to turn the dial.*

LEON: What shall we get? The news!

(See film still 17.)

NINOTCHKA: No, no news. We don't want to know what's happening in the world. We want to be left alone, don't we?

LEON: Yes, sweetheart . . . all by ourselves.

NINOTCHKA *(remembering vaguely)*: Well, then we turn twice to the right and stop at seven . . .

LEON *follows her instructions.*

[NINOTCHKA *(after a little pause, sadly)*: It's dead.

LEON: Well, it has to warm up . . . you have to give it a chance . . . just like people . . . like you and me . . . first you wanted to fight me and now we belong to the same party . . . salute!

He takes her in his arms and again they embrace.

NINOTCHKA *(as though she were in heaven)*: Now twice to the left and stop at seventeen.

LEON *again follows her instructions.*]

Interior—Safe, *shooting toward the door.*

LEON *opens the door and both look into the safe.*

NINOTCHKA *(disappointed)*: No music.

LEON *(also disappointed)*: No, no music.

Through her fog, NINOTCHKA *becomes aware of the case containing the jewels.*

NINOTCHKA *(bitterly)*: There it is . . . Thursday . . . you can't rip it out of the week. . . .

LEON *(helpfully)*: But I can throw it out of the window.

NINOTCHKA *(philosophically)*: It wouldn't be fair to the man in the street. *(She pushes back the lid)* There they are . . . they are terrible things, those jewels. . . .

LEON: . . . but big.

NINOTCHKA: . . . they are the tears of Old Russia . . . see that stone?

LEON: Who cried that one?

NINOTCHKA: Czar Peter gave it to his wife, Catherine the Great. For it he sold ten thousand serfs in the market.

LEON: Now, darling, don't get impatient, wait until we are married.

76

You know that worthless butler of mine . . . that reactionary? Some day when I come home to you I may say, "Darling, I drove Gaston to the market and look what I got from him!"

From the case of jewels he takes a beautiful diadem and holds it in front of her.

[NINOTCHKA *(the economist now)*: First ten thousand serfs . . . now just Gaston. It is very encouraging.]

LEON *takes her by the hand and leads her from the safe.*

LEON: Come, sweetheart. Let me put it on you. You will teach these jewels. For the first time they will learn how they can look.

NINOTCHKA: They belong to the people.

LEON *(in a ceremonial voice)*: I give them back to the people . . . *(As formal and steady as possible under the conditions he puts the diadem on her head)* I make you Ninotchka the Great . . . Duchess of the People! . . . Grand Duchess of the People!

NINOTCHKA *falls in with the spirit of this imaginary coronation.*

NINOTCHKA: Is this the wish of the masses?

LEON: It is their wish.

NINOTCHKA: Thank you, Leon . . . thank you, masses. *(In a low voice)* Can I make a speech now?

LEON: Please.

NINOTCHKA *turns to an imaginary assemblage.*

NINOTCHKA: Comrades! People of the world! The revolution is on the march . . . I know . . . wars will wash over us . . . bombs will fall . . . all civilization will crumble . . . but not yet, please . . . wait, wait . . . what's the hurry? *(Mixing reality with fantasy)* Let us be happy . . . give us our moment. . . . *(Turning to LEON)* We are happy, aren't we, Leon?

LEON *(fondly)*: Yes, sweetheart. *(He holds her in his arms)*

NINOTCHKA: *(Her voice getting dimmer and dimmer)*: So happy and so tired.

She falls asleep in his arms. LEON gathers her up and carries her into the bedroom, the diadem still on her head.

Bedroom—the Royal Suite

LEON *carries* NINOTCHKA *to the bed, puts her down on it. She is now sleeping soundly. He kisses her once more and then turns, the* CAMERA PANNING *with him, and starts toward the door to the corridor and exits. As he closes the door with an uncertain hand, it slams.*

Close Shot—Ninotchka, *as she lies on the bed. On the night table beside her is a photograph of the stern-faced Lenin. The crash of the slamming door awakens* NINOTCHKA *for a moment. Completely content and happy, she turns around and sees the disapproving face of the photograph.*

NINOTCHKA *(charmingly)*: Smile, little father, smile.

Insert of Photograph of Lenin

The photograph of Lenin starts to smile in approval, as we . . .

Fade out

Fade in on:

An Establishing Shot of Paris—Day

In the foreground a clock shows that it is a quarter to twelve.

Dissolve to:

Long Shot—Living Room of the Royal Suite

It is taken from an ANGLE *which includes the door. The lights are still on, the curtains drawn, the empty champagne bottle and glasses litter the room. We hear the buzzer of the corridor door ring several times without an answer.*

78

CAMERA MOVES *through the door into the bedroom, never disclosing the bed. The lights in the bedroom are still lighted also and the curtains drawn.* CAMERA STOPS *on the door from the bedroom to the corridor. The buzzer rings. Apparently the caller has moved from the living-room door to the bedroom door.*

Close Shot of the Bed

NINOTCHKA *is lying on the bed, still in her evening dress. The diadem is no longer on her head, but no special emphasis is laid on that detail in the camera angle. We hear the sound of the buzzer ringing again and again.* NINOTCHKA *half wakens and calls out something which sounds like "come in" without being fully aware of what she is doing.*

Bedroom—at the Door

The door is opened from the outside by a maid, who lets in the DUCHESS SWANA, *dressed in a smart morning outfit.* SWANA *looks around, surprised and amused at the state of the room. She walks over to the bed where lies* NINOTCHKA, *still not enough awake to face reality.* SWANA *is delighted to have surprised* NINOTCHKA *in this condition.*

SWANA *(ironically)*: Good morning.

NINOTCHKA *(awakening gradually)*: What?

SWANA: It is tomorrow morning . . . tomorrow noon, to be exact. I hope you will forgive me. I know it's extremely cruel to waken anyone at such an hour. Don't you recognize me? I am the Duchess Swana.

By now NINOTCHKA *is awake. She gets up and realizes to her acute embarrassment the condition in which* SWANA *has found her.*

SWANA: I know how you feel, my dear. The morning after always does look grim if you happen to be wearing last night's dress. Don't be embarrassed by my presence, though. You couldn't have found anybody more sympathetic to your condition. [I remember once in Petrograd when I felt exactly as you do. I had to bow from a balcony to the crowd. My dear, the masses have no understanding of the feelings of a lady before noon. Don't you find that true?]

> *During* SWANA's *speech* NINOTCHKA *has found herself completely.*

NINOTCHKA: I think we can cut your visit short. Leon is not here. *(See film still 18.)*

SWANA: Of course not, my dear! I didn't come here with any such suspicion. How ridiculous! *(With a glance toward the living room)* Nor did I come here to pick up his hat.

Close Shot—Leon's Hat, *shot through the bedroom door into the living room where it lies on the table.*

Long Shot—Living Room—Toward Bedroom Door

> *By the bed stand* NINOTCHKA *and* SWANA. SWANA *starts toward the living room,* NINOTCHKA *following her.*

[SWANA *(as she reaches the threshold)*: How stale last night's gaiety looks! It has the taste of a dead cigarette.

NINOTCHKA: If you were encouraged to come here by our meeting last night I am afraid you misunderstood my attitude.

SWANA: Don't worry, you were quite rude enough. *(During the following speech, she draws the curtains and opens the windows)* Do you mind if I let in a little fresh air and sunshine? I'm sure it will make you feel better and I want you to be at your very best. In full possession of your faculties, at least.

NINOTCHKA *(regaining her usual firmness)*: Please come to the point. What is it you want?

80

SWANA: I just dropped in to have a little heart-to-heart talk with you.

NINOTCHKA: We have nothing to discuss.

SWANA: Now there you are completely wrong. If we sit down for a little chat, I'm sure we won't run out of conversation and what's more it won't be dull.]

NINOTCHKA: Madame, what is it you people always say, regardless of what you mean . . . "I am delighted to have you here"? I have not reached that stage of civilization.

[SWANA: That's all right . . . I grow on people.]

NINOTCHKA: I must ask you to leave.

SWANA: Leave? That's exactly what I came here to ask *you* to do. Leave! I don't mean this hotel and I don't mean Paris . . . I mean France. There's a plane for Moscow at five-forty.

[NINOTCHKA *(puzzled)*: Madame, if you . . .

SWANA: Don't worry. I have already made reservations. It's perfect flying weather. They assure me there's a fine tail wind which will sweep you back to Moscow in no time.

NINOTCHKA *(still not understanding)*: If this is meant to be a joke it is not funny. Or] do you still think you're issuing orders from your palace in Petrograd?

> NINOTCHKA's *words for the first time sting* SWANA *out of her apparently superficial attitude.*

SWANA *(bitterly)*: My palace in Petrograd . . . yes, you took that away from me. You took away my czar, my country, my people, everything I had . . . *(With emphasis)* but nothing more—I warn you.

NINOTCHKA *(simply)*: People cannot be taken away, madame, neither a hundred and sixty million nor one. Not if you have their love. You hadn't. That's why you're not in Russia any longer, and that's why you came here this morning.

[SWANA: Very interesting, my dear, but couldn't you write all that from Moscow? A dissertation on love on Soviet stationery—would be an amusing paradox.

NINOTCHKA: It is not enough to be witty, madame. People grow tired of being entertained. You made that mistake before.] Problems were never solved by bowing from a balcony.

SWANA: My dear, you don't know how impressive I could be. Did you ever see me in my regalia with my diadem and all my jewels?

The word diadem startles NINOTCHKA. *She starts to remember the night before, and she looks toward the safe.*

Insert of the Door of the Safe, *which is closed by now.*

[Close Shot—Ninotchka and Swana

NINOTCHKA *stares in the direction of the safe as* SWANA *chatters on.*

SWANA: You can't deny we gave the people their money's worth—almost—eight tumbling Romanoffs—eight!

NINOTCHKA *(desperately)*: I must insist that you leave.

SWANA: Not before you agree to use those reservations to Moscow.

NINOTCHKA: In that case I can only say good-by.

Abruptly she walks toward the bedroom.]

Traveling Shot of Ninotchka

She enters the small room connecting the living room and bedroom and closes the door to the living room. She walks into the bedroom toward the bed and glances at it. The diadem is not there. After going back into the anteroom, she opens the outer door of the safe and pulls on the inner door. It has not been properly closed and opens at once. The safe is empty. NINOTCHKA *stands staring in frozen horror for a moment, then rushes to the telephone by the bed.*

NINOTCHKA *(into the telephone)*: Élysée 2763.

Long Shot—Ninotchka at the Telephone, *waiting for her connection. In the background the door to the living room is opened by* SWANA.

[SWANA *(standing in the door)*: I wouldn't waken Leon. After last night I would say not before three o'clock at the earliest.

NINOTCHKA: I told you to go, madame.]

SWANA: Believe me, Leon can't help you. He doesn't know anything about the jewels . . . I give you my word . . . I swear it.

NINOTCHKA *hangs up the receiver and stares at* SWANA. *She walks toward her.*

Living Room, *shooting into the bedroom. In the foreground* SWANA, *in the background* NINOTCHKA, *who is hurrying toward her.*

NINOTCHKA: Where are they?

SWANA: You were very careless with our precious jewels, my dear. They're too expensive a toy for two children to play with.

NINOTCHKA: Where are they?

SWANA: Don't worry. Fortunately last night a very trustworthy friend kept his eyes open. Perhaps he overstepped his function as a waiter but he fulfilled his duty as a Russian. *(She draws back the fur scarf she is wearing, revealing a diamond star, one of the jewels we have seen)* I just put this on for sentiment. The rest are absolutely safe. I assure you. But if you feel like notifying the police . . .

NINOTCHKA: You leave me no choice.

SWANA: Won't it be rather embarrassing for a Soviet Envoy to disclose the circumstances under which she lost them?

NINOTCHKA: I will have to face the consequences, but so will you. Don't forget they will ask how you got them.

SWANA: That's very simple to answer. They were given to me by my mother. They were given to her by her mother, in fact they're mine, you cannot steal what belongs to you!

She proceeds into the living room, followed by NINOTCHKA.

83

NINOTCHKA: They always belonged to the Russian people. They were paid for with their sweat, their blood, their lives and you will give them back!

SWANA *(triumphantly)*: I told you we had plenty to talk about. Shall we sit down?

They both sit.

SWANA *(very matter-of-fact)*: Now, let's free ourselves from emotionalism and try to solve the problem in a practical way. Our situation has changed considerably. Before I had only a claim to the jewels. Now I have the jewels.

NINOTCHKA: In other words moral ideas have no weight with you . . . all right, then let's deal with legal facts. You know that France has recognized the Soviet.

SWANA: Unfortunately.

NINOTCHKA: Under Soviet law the jewels belong to the State. France is going to uphold that ownership.

SWANA: My lawyer agrees with you. He says France will uphold it in every court, but I will drag you through every court, don't forget that. And when I say it will take two years I am, as always, conservative.

NINOTCHKA: Won't those two years in court be expensive for you? I know that money was no object as long as you could squeeze it from the pockets of the people, but now . . .

SWANA: I may run out of money, but you have already run out of bread. Two years is a long time for your comrades to wait.

NINOTCHKA: I see. You have calculated in terms of hunger.

SWANA: No, I just wanted to be absolutely impartial. Both of us are faced with two rather uncomfortable years. We can condense these two years to two minutes if you want to accept my proposition.

NINOTCHKA *now realizes what she is after.*

NINOTCHKA: Go on.

SWANA: I am willing to hand over the jewels and sign the necessary papers if you take that five-forty plane to Moscow.

NINOTCHKA *(quietly)*: That's not the way to win him back . . . not Leon.

SWANA: I think I know Leon quite as well as you . . . possibly a little better. Leave that worry to me. Five-forty leaves you time enough to close the deal with Monsieur Mercier, but naturally you'll be too busy for any farewells. I'll see to it that everything is done in the most expeditious manner and I will also see you to the airport. That's my proposition, Comrade Yakushova.

> NINOTCHKA *knows herself to be faced with an inevitable decision. For a moment she cannot answer. The telephone rings.* NINOTCHKA *takes the receiver.*

NINOTCHKA *(into telephone)*: Yes . . . *(It is* LEON*)* Oh hello . . . *Much as she wants to talk to him she hesitates in the presence of* SWANA. SWANA *realizes the situation, gets up, and walks over to the window, where she stands looking out.*

Close-up—Ninotchka at Telephone

NINOTCHKA: Good morning, Leon . . . *(Forcing herself to be gay so that he will not suspect anything)* . . . no, you didn't waken me . . . I am fine, thank you. . . . Yes, it was . . . marvelous. . . . What? . . . for luncheon? I'm afraid I can't. I am going to be very busy . . . *(Looking for excuses)* well, I have a lot of things to attend to today. . . . What? . . . Well to tell you the truth I am a little tired and I would like to rest . . . *(She forces herself to laugh)* you may be right . . . perhaps it is the champagne. . . . For dinner? . . . Of course . . . seven o'clock here? . . . *(Realizing that she will be gone by then)* seven o'clock is all right. . . . Where? . . . That will be lovely. . . . Yes . . . *(There is a knock on the door)* Come in. *(Into the telephone)* Yes? . . . *(Looking toward the door she sees something which makes her stop the conversation)* Just a moment. . . . *(She puts the receiver on the table and walks toward the door)*

Anteroom between Living Room and Corridor, *shooting toward the living room. In the background we see* SWANA *standing at the window.* NINOTCHKA *comes into the anteroom, closes the door in order to shut off* SWANA'S *view.* CAMERA PANS *with* NINOTCHKA *as she walks toward the hall door where the bellboy is putting down a big flower basket.*

NINOTCHKA *(to bellboy)*: You can leave it here.

The bellboy exits. NINOTCHKA *looks at the basket of flowers for a moment, then takes the envelope which is attached to the handle. She opens it and reads the enclosed letter. It must be a love note, for her eyes grow wet. She turns to the last page.*

Insert

". . . and sweetheart, I have kept my first promise. I sent poor old Gaston to the market this morning and if you will look deep into the flowers you will see what I got for him. . . ."

Close Shot—Ninotchka

She puts her hand in the basket and takes out a bottle of milk.

Insert of the Bottle

On the label we see a picture of a goat.

Ninotchka

She smiles sadly and goes to the telephone, which is on the console in the anteroom.

NINOTCHKA *(into telephone)*: Operator, will you switch the call please? . . . Hello? . . . Darling, your present just arrived. . . . It's very silly and very wonderful . . . thank you. . . . No, I

won't forget . . . seven o'clock. . . . *(With great tenderness)*
Good-by, my darling. . . . What? . . . Oh . . . *(softly)* salute!
She puts down the receiver. CAMERA PANS *with her as she goes to the door of the living room. She opens the door and goes in.* SWANA *turns from the window.*
NINOTCHKA: I am sorry to have kept you waiting, madame.

Dissolve to:
[**Swana—at the Airport,** *shooting from a* HIGH ANGLE. *We hear the* SOUND *of an airplane just taking off.* CAMERA PULLS BACK *so that* SWANA *seems to be photographed from the airplane. Finally the* SHOT *discloses the whole airport and* SWANA *disappearing into the crowd.*]

Entrance Hall—Swana's Apartment
SWANA'*s maid is opening the door for* SWANA, *who enters in the highest spirits.*
SWANA: Good afternoon, Jacqueline.
MAID: Good afternoon, Your Highness. *(Hesitantly)* Madame, I . . .
SWANA: You didn't find my glove. All right, you're forgiven.
MAID: Thank you, Your Highness. Count d'Algout is waiting. He's been here some time.
SWANA *inspects herself briefly in the hall mirror, proceeds into the living room.*

Living Room—Swana's Apartment
LEON *is pacing up and down.* SWANA *enters.*
SWANA: Leon, darling, how nice! Have you ordered tea or a cocktail?
LEON: No thanks, Swana.

SWANA: Did I act stupidly last night? Should I apologize?

LEON: I'm the one who should apologize. I should have talked to you before.

SWANA: Is this, by any chance, going to be a confession?

LEON: Yes.

SWANA: Oh, no, my little Volga boatman. Have you forgotten our First Commandment: Never Complain—Never Explain. It has worked so often and so perfectly, don't let's break the rule. And please don't look so guilty, otherwise I'll . . .

LEON: This time, Swana—just this once—I must ask you to listen.

SWANA: All right, I'll listen.

LEON: I know you hate the obvious but do you mind if, at this moment, I'm not in the least subtle?

SWANA: Brutal frankness, if you insist.

LEON: There are a hundred ways to approach it, but I feel it can best be said in one simple phrase. I'm in love, Swana.

(See film still 19.)

SWANA: And I thought it was something serious! How could you frighten me so?

LEON: It must be serious, Swana. Not long ago I'd have considered such a statement rather juvenile and rather middle class. Now I can say it without stammering, without a blush. I'm in love, Swana.

[SWANA: Say it over and over again, Leon. Words are a wonderful safety valve, and that's what you need—because you know it's impossible, don't you?

LEON: I have to be simple again, Swana, and you may find it shockingly banal. I've thought it over and I'm willing to take all the consequences, even if it means a complete readjustment of my way of living.]

SWANA: Leon! This has the ugly sound of regeneration.

LEON: I'm afraid that's what it is.

SWANA: The same old trouble, Leon. You're always late. Whether you're taking me to the Opera or calling for me at a beauty shop, you're never on time. And now, when it's a question of your reform—late again. *(She glances at her wrist watch)* By about five minutes.

LEON: What is this, Swana?

SWANA: Knowing the efficiency of the French Air Service I think I can guarantee that Madame Yakushova has already taken off for Moscow.

LEON: Has done what?

SWANA: She's gone, Leon.

LEON: Do you expect me to believe that?

> SWANA *picks up the receiver of the telephone and holds it out to him.*

SWANA: Here's the telephone. If you call the hotel you will find that you have no seven o'clock appointment.

The Moscow Plane
> *It is flying past the Eiffel Tower.*

Close Shot—Airplane Window
> *Behind the window we see* NINOTCHKA *looking at Paris for the last time.* CAMERA MOVES OVER *to the next window and we see* BULJANOFF, IRANOFF, *and* KOPALSKI *also giving Paris a sad farewell look.*

Another View of Paris, *from the air. The mist has closed in by now so that only the top of the Eiffel Tower is visible above it.*

Close-up—Ninotchka, *looking down on the Tower.*

Interior, Airplane—Ninotchka, Buljanoff, Iranoff, and Kopalski
> NINOTCHKA *turns from the window and leans against the back of her chair. The* RUSSIANS *follow her example. There is a moment of silence and sadness.*

89

BULJANOFF: Imagine, for once in our lives we were in Paris and we never went to the Eiffel Tower.

KOPALSKI: That's right.

IRANOFF: They tell me it has a wonderful restaurant on the second floor.

[KOPALSKI: While you eat, you look at the view.]

Close-up—Ninotchka

She is trying to overcome all sentimentality, but as the following speech progresses she cannot escape the personal implication involved.

NINOTCHKA: Yes, it is an amazing piece of engineering. Still the most remarkable iron structure in the world. Leading to the top there is a staircase of over a thousand steps . . . but an elevator is included in the price of admission.

Fade out

[**Fade in:**
Insert of a Paris Newspaper
HERALD DU MATIN
CAMERA ZOOMS DOWN *on a headline of an article.*
MERCIER BUYS PRICELESS RUSSIAN
JEWELS. RUSSIAN COMMISSION HAS
LEFT FOR MOSCOW.

Street in Paris—Morning

CAMERA FOLLOWS LEON *as he walks excitedly and nervously along the boulevard. He turns into a Russian Intouriste Bureau, one of the travel bureaus maintained by the Soviet government in foreign countries to supply information regarding travel, give visas, etc.*]

90

Intouriste Bureau

It is a typical travel bureau. Behind the counter are attendants and some people getting information and pamphlets. LEON *enters, looks around, and sees a door which says* "VISAS AND PASSPORT DEPARTMENT." *He enters.*

Interior, Visa Room

It is a room smaller than the previous one. Behind the counter stands a typical Bolshevik OFFICIAL. *In front of the counter is an elderly English lady.* LEON *takes his place behind her, nervous at having to wait. The* OFFICIAL *stamps the English lady's passport and hands it to her.*

OFFICIAL: Well, everything is in order. I hope you will enjoy your trip to Russia, madame.

ENGLISH LADY: Thank you. Oh, by the way, I've heard so many rumors about laundry conditions in Russia. Is it advisable to take one's own towels?

OFFICIAL: Certainly not, madame. That's only capitalistic propaganda. We change the towel every week.

ENGLISH LADY: Oh . . . thank you.

She leaves. LEON *moves up to the* OFFICIAL.

OFFICIAL: Yes, please?

At this moment the telephone rings. The OFFICIAL *takes the receiver.*

OFFICIAL *(into phone)*: Yes . . . Comrade Cazabine? No, I'm sorry . . . he hasn't been with us for six months. He was called back to Russia and was investigated. You can get further details from his widow.

He hangs up the receiver. LEON, *thinking of* NINOTCHKA, *is horrified by this statement.*

LEON: Pardon me, I am very interested in what you just said— you mean when an envoy goes back to Russia—if they don't like what he has done they put him out of the way?

OFFICIAL: Not always . . . look at me . . . I've been back twice. *(He knocks on wood)*

LEON *(his alarm growing)*: Here's my passport. . . . Please give me a visa. I have to leave for Russia immediately.

OFFICIAL *(reading passport)*: Count Leon d'Algout . . . a count! . . . a nobleman!

LEON: Don't hold that against me . . . please!

OFFICIAL: Why should an aristocrat want to go to Russia?

LEON: Business.

OFFICIAL: What business?

LEON: Private.

OFFICIAL: There is no privacy in Russia. This whole thing seems very suspicious. What's the real reason? If you ever want to get into Russia, take my advice . . . confess!

[LEON *(dismayed)*: Confess what?

OFFICIAL: Are you sympathetic to the former Czaristic government—the White Russians?

LEON: On the contrary—I don't want to have anything to do with them.

OFFICIAL: You believe in our cause?

> LEON, *feeling that he has to go to the rescue of his girl, whips up an enormous enthusiasm for the cause.*

LEON: Oh . . . I think it's great! Everyone works—everyone contributes—that's what I want to do—work! I make my own bed— you can call up my butler! I don't believe in the right of the individual. I like the Bolshevik ideal—everyone being the same. You just like me—me just like you—I use your comb—you use my toothbrush—oh, it's a great life. . . . Please . . . give me that visa!

> *At this moment* SWANA *enters.*

SWANA: Hello, Leon darling!

LEON *(startled)*: Hello.

SWANA *(suavely)* After our talk last night I took it for granted that you would drop in here this morning. Knowing how difficult it is to get into Soviet Russia, I thought I might be of some assistance to you. *(To the* OFFICIAL*)* May I introduce myself? I am the Duchess Swana of Russia . . . another Russia.

The OFFICIAL *gasps in surprise.*

LEON: Now, please, Swana.

SWANA *(to the* OFFICIAL*)*: Count d'Algout was for several years my personal representative and if it is necessary to sign any affidavit for him I'll be delighted.

LEON *(bitterly)*: That does it, Swana. *(He leads her toward the door)* Now you mustn't miss your appointment with your hairdresser.

SWANA *(stopping at the door)*: Just in case they don't give you your visa to Russia I want you to know that I have signed a contract for my memoirs and rented a lovely little château in the Touraine, and if you feel the need of a change . . .

LEON: Thank you, Swana. You are very gracious.

His words are unmistakably a final dismissal. She walks out. LEON *looks after her for a second, then goes back to the* OFFICIAL. *He tries to laugh off the incident.*

LEON: She must have her little joke. *(The* OFFICIAL *responds with a stony look)* You're not going to take that seriously.

OFFICIAL: The Grand Duchess Swana . . . active in the White Russian movement?

LEON: Believe me, I have no connection with her any longer . . . I swear I haven't!

OFFICIAL: But you had!]

LEON: Listen, I want to be absolutely frank with you. I have no business in Moscow.

OFFICIAL: I think so too.

LEON: I want to see a friend of mine . . . a very dear friend. . . . It's a personal matter which has nothing to do with politics or social philosophies. . . . It's a girl.

OFFICIAL: So it's love which drags you to Moscow.

LEON: Yes!

OFFICIAL: No visa.

LEON *(fighting for his point)*: I *must* get into that country of yours!

OFFICIAL: Oh no. No visa.

LEON *(more aggressively)*: That's impossible! Nobody has the right. . . . You can't do that! . . . If you don't give me that visa . . .

OFFICIAL *(ironically)*: You're going to force us . . . huh?

LEON *(growing violent)*: Now look here . . . you advertise all over the world that you want people to go into your country and when someone tries to get in, you keep him out!

OFFICIAL: Why should I take a chance?

LEON: On what?

OFFICIAL: How do I know you don't want to blow up a factory?

LEON: What for . . . why?

OFFICIAL: Or a tunnel or a bridge . . .

LEON: Suspicions . . . nothing but suspicions! . . . That's the trouble with you! If you don't let me in I'll stand in front of this office of yours and warn people to keep away from Russia! . . . I'll picket your whole country. . . .

The OFFICIAL *laughs in a superior way.*

LEON: I'll boycott you, that's what I'm going to do! . . . No more vodka . . . no more caviar . . . no more Tchaikovsky . . . no more borscht. . . . Wait a minute, I know something better than that. . . .

The OFFICIAL *leans forward sarcastically.*

OFFICIAL: What?

With a knock-out blow, LEON *sends him to the floor, then, leaning over the counter, he shouts.*

LEON: And you can tell the Kremlin that's just the beginning!

He strides out.

The OFFICIAL'*s head emerges from the counter. As he adjusts his bruised jaw, he speaks.*

OFFICIAL: No visa.

Fade in on:
Establishing Shot of Russia—First of May—Stock Shot of May Day Parade on the Red Square
(See film still 20.)

Dissolve to:
Radio Announcer
RADIO ANNOUNCER: March, march, march! Comrades of the World, never has there been such a May Day parade as this! Already for four hours the pavements of Moscow have resounded to the tread of a million boots! Thousands of gun-carriages have thundered past. Thousands of tanks, combined with our mighty air force, have demonstrated to a belligerent neighbor that we are ready and invincible! Now past me marches the great army of our civilians! Men and women of all ages. All servants of the State united in one thought and ideal.

Group of Several Units Marching
Workmen, soldiers, tanks, airplanes, etc.

Dissolve to:

Column of Women, *dressed in typical Russian May Day parade fashion, marching and saluting. The* CAMERA NARROWS DOWN *to a* CLOSE SHOT OF NINOTCHKA *marching with the others. All her individuality is gone. She is one of many, a cog in the Russian machine. With a stern expression she is looking*

95

straight ahead [*when suddenly something attracts her attention and she glances to one side.*
(See film still 21.)

A Column of Male Workers *is coming in the opposite direction.* BULJANOFF, IRANOFF, *and* KOPALSKI *are recognizable among them.*

Close Shot—Buljanoff, Iranoff, and Kopalski *marching. All three are already pretty exhausted from the long march.* KOPALSKI *sees* NINOTCHKA. *He whispers it to the others. The three look toward* NINOTCHKA *and lift their shoulders with a gesture which says, "Look where we are now."*

Close Shot—Ninotchka, *answering them with a sad smile. After they have passed she stares straight forward again with the same stern expression.*]

Dissolve to:

Panning Shot—Staircase in Ninotchka's Tenement House
It is an overcrowded house. People are walking up and down stairs, standing grouped in front of the various apartments; children are sliding down the banisters and playing games under the feet of the adults.

NINOTCHKA *trudges upstairs wearily.* CAMERA PANS *with her as she goes into an apartment which is divided into several sub-apartments. Finally she opens the door of her own room and goes in.*

Ninotchka's Room

It is a comparatively small room, which she shares with two other girls. As she enters only one girl is present. It is ANNA, *a cello player, who sits on the edge of her bed practicing on her cello. Apparently* NINOTCHKA *has not adjusted herself completely to the Moscow which she once thought so great.*

NINOTCHKA: Good evening, Anna.

ANNA: Good evening, Ninotchka.

NINOTCHKA: Aren't you late?

ANNA: No, the opera starts an hour later tonight on account of the parade.

During the following scene ANNA *puts her cello in its case and gets ready to go to her job.* NINOTCHKA *starts to arrange the table in the center of the floor for a party of four. Out of her cupboard she takes very primitive-looking dishes, a flower pot, glasses, and a kind of shawl which serves as a tablecloth.*

NINOTCHKA: Didn't you march?

ANNA *is apparently not a fanatical believer in the Bolshevik regime and takes a cynical and humorous attitude toward it.*

ANNA: They didn't let me. I am in disgrace. Last week at the performance of *Carmen* I played a sour note. The conductor got so excited he yelled, "There's sabotage in the string section!"

NINOTCHKA: Too bad . . . you missed an inspiring day, Anna. *(See film still 22.)*

ANNA: I know . . . [my heart is sad . . . but my feet are happy. When all the tanks and guns were roaring over the Red Square I sat here all by myself and played a Beethoven sonata. Not bad at all.] *(She has noticed* NINOTCHKA'S *preparations)* Are you expecting someone?

NINOTCHKA: A few friends . . . just a little dinner party.

ANNA: What are you serving?

NINOTCHKA: An omelet.

ANNA *(puzzled)*: An omelet! Aren't you living a little above your ration?

NINOTCHKA: Well, I've saved up two eggs and each of my friends is bringing his own so we'll manage.

ANNA: It just goes to prove the theory of our State. If you stand alone it means a boiled egg but if you're true to the collective spirit and stick together you've got an omelet. *(Devilishly)* That reminds me . . . have you heard the latest they're telling about the Kremlin?

At this moment a door to one of the adjoining rooms opens and GURGANOV, *a middle-aged man with a sour stool-pigeon expression, walks quietly through the room to another door, taking in the girls with one sly glance and giving the impression that not only his eyes but his ears are open.* ANNA *breaks off her remark.*

ANNA *(whispering)*: I'll tell you later. *(After* GURGANOV *has disappeared into the other room she continues)* That Gurganov, you never know whether he's on his way to the washroom or the Secret Police.

NINOTCHKA: You should be more careful, Anna.

ANNA: And you too, Ninotchka.

NINOTCHKA *(amazed)*: About what?

ANNA: Ever since you have been back from Paris . . .

NINOTCHKA: I haven't talked to anyone about Paris. I haven't said a word.

ANNA: That's just it. It makes people feel queer. I don't want you to get in any trouble.

NINOTCHKA: I have nothing to hide.

ANNA: You should. I'll show you.

She walks over to her cupboard and takes out a piece of lingerie and comes back to NINOTCHKA *with it.*

ANNA: When I passed through the laundry yard today I saw all the women huddled around this so I brought it up here. Things like this create a bad feeling. First they didn't know whose it was. Then they saw the Paris label and did it start a commotion! Some said it's what we all ought to wear and others said it's like hanging foreign ideas on our clothesline. It undermines our whole cause.

NINOTCHKA *(aware of the pettiness which surrounds her)*: I see.

ANNA: You know how it is today . . . all you have to do is wear a pair of silk stockings and they suspect you of counter-revolution.

NINOTCHKA: Thank you, Anna. I'll dry it up here when I wash it next. I should hate to see our country endangered by my underwear.

ANNA *(confidentially)*: Ninotchka, you know I am your friend, you can trust me. . . . Did you bring back anything else?

NINOTCHKA *suddenly is transported to Paris in her memory.*

NINOTCHKA *(with feeling)*: No, I left everything in Paris. I just happened to be wearing this.

ANNA: Tell me . . . what else did you have?

NINOTCHKA *(enjoying the thought)*: Well, a hat . . .

ANNA: What was it like?

NINOTCHKA: It was very silly. . . . I would be ashamed to wear it here.

ANNA: As beautiful as that? What else? Come, tell me.

NINOTCHKA: An evening gown.

ANNA *(puzzled)*: Evening gown?

NINOTCHKA: A dress you wear in the evening.

ANNA: What do you wear in the morning?

NINOTCHKA: When you get up you put on a negligee, and then you change to a morning frock.

ANNA: You mean to tell me you wear a different dress for different times of the day?

NINOTCHKA: Yes.

ANNA: Now, Ninotchka, you're exaggerating.

NINOTCHKA: No, my dear, it is true. That's how they live in the other world. Here we dress to have our bodies covered . . . to keep warm. . . .

ANNA: And there?

NINOTCHKA: Well, sometimes they're not completely covered but . . . they don't freeze.

ANNA (*fingering the piece of lingerie*): They must have wonderful materials to make a thing like this so soft . . . something you don't even see.

NINOTCHKA: You feel it, though.

ANNA (*hesitantly*): Ninotchka, I wouldn't bring this up if we weren't such good friends.

NINOTCHKA: What is it, Anna?

ANNA: You know I told you that Pavlov and I are going to get married when he comes back from the maneuvers. Would it be asking too much . . .

NINOTCHKA: You want this?

ANNA: Just for the honeymoon.

NINOTCHKA: You can have it for good. It is my wedding present.
(See film still 23.)

ANNA *is for a moment speechless over this generous gift. She embraces and kisses* NINOTCHKA.

ANNA: Ninotchka! Ninotchka!

She kisses her again, takes her cello, and starts to leave.

ANNA: Am I going to play that cadenza tonight!

ANNA *exits, closing the door.* NINOTCHKA *is left alone. Her thoughts are still in the other world, obviously with* LEON. *Mechanically she looks over the table to see if everything is all right, then she walks over to the radio (a primitive little machine). As she turns the knob she smiles again reminiscently. As she does, the blare of a Russian speech brings her back to reality.*

VOICE ON RADIO: Individuals? Yes, as atoms in the cosmos of Soviet Russia. [Family? Yes. One great family of one hundred and sixty million, struggling, fighting, victorious Russian proletarians. Thus shall we pursue our way into the future, fists clenched, hearts encased in steel armed against bourgeois sentimentality and . . .]

Quickly she turns the knob and again there is a burst of Russian oratory.

SECOND VOICE ON RADIO: . . . [From the Exploiters for the

100

Toilers. We are going full steam ahead through industrialization toward socialism. Let us put the Union of Socialistic Soviet Re-publics] into an automobile and the muzhik into a tractor, and then let the capitalists try to keep up with us!

The same thing happens for a third time.

THIRD VOICE ON RADIO: . . . and thirty million peasants, eighty-five per cent of the population [owned three hundred forty-three million four hundred and sixty-nine thousand acres of land, sixty-five per cent of the total area. And one hundred and fifty thousand nobles possessed thirty-five per cent of the country's natural wealth!]

NINOTCHKA *turns off the radio. She closes her eyes for a moment and with a sad smile murmurs to herself.*

NINOTCHKA: No music.

At this moment the door opens, and BULJANOFF, IRANOFF, *and* KOPALSKI *enter. There follow warm greetings between* NINOTCHKA *and the* THREE RUSSIANS.

ALL THREE RUSSIANS: Ninotchka! Ninotchka!

A moment of silence follows. The four look at each other as people do who share a secret.

NINOTCHKA *(with great warmth)*: How are you, you three scoundrels?

KOPALSKI *(wryly)*: Well, we're back home.

BULJANOFF *(sourly)*: You know what they say—there's nothing like home.

IRANOFF: That's right . . . and we might as well face it.

NINOTCHKA *(trying not to say what she feels)*: Come, now, you must not talk that way. . . . You have to adjust yourselves. . . . We must be brave.

IRANOFF: Brave . . . that's right.

BULJANOFF: Let's be happy that we're all alive.

IRANOFF: And that's something we owe to Ninotchka.

KOPALSKI: If you hadn't given Commissar Razinin such a wonderful report about us, who knows what would have happened?

101

BULJANOFF: I can tell you exactly.

NINOTCHKA: Now let's forget everything except that we're together.
[BULJANOFF: That's right.]

IRANOFF: Let's do that.

KOPALSKI *(falling in with her attempt)*: It's a real Paris reunion.

IRANOFF: If you close your eyes and listen to our voices we might be in Paris.

NINOTCHKA: Let's not close our eyes. There are many good things to see here too.

[BULJANOFF *(cynically)*: I think I need my glasses.

KOPALSKI *(reprimanding him quietly)*: A little more tact . . .]
look how nicely she's fixed the table—all for us.

[BULJANOFF *(in a loud voice, trying to make up for his faux pas)*:
How nicely you've fixed the table, Ninotchka.]

IRANOFF: What a lovely room you have here.

BULJANOFF: How many families live here with you?

NINOTCHKA: Only myself and two other girls. One is a cello player in the opera and the other a street-car conductor.

IRANOFF *(impressed)*: Just three people in a room this size? Whew!

KOPALSKI *(inspecting the room)*: [And your own gas cooker?
That's marvelous! *(Forgetting himself)* Naturally it's not the Royal Suite . . .]³⁶

NINOTCHKA: Sssh! Once and for all, we're in Moscow!

KOPALSKI *(walking over to the window)*: Yes, there's no doubt of that. . . . *(Sarcastically)* Just look out of the window and there it is.

NINOTCHKA: And it's great! Think what it was a few years ago and what it is now.

> IRANOFF *and* BULJANOFF *have joined them at the window.*

---

³⁶ In the film, instead:
BULJANOFF: And your own radio. Look here—isn't that wonderful?
IRANOFF: Look at this—what good material.
KOPALSKI: Naturally, it's not the Royal Suite.

IRANOFF: She's right . . . *(Under his breath)* anyhow let's talk ourselves into it.

BULJANOFF: Just see how happy the people look . . . from here. . . .

KOPALSKI: Can you blame them? . . . at least the May Day parade is over.

BULJANOFF: That's another thing . . . it's spring.

NINOTCHKA: The same spring we had in Paris. Just as good.

KOPALSKI: Even the swallows are back.

BULJANOFF AND IRANOFF: Yes, that's right.

IRANOFF: Maybe that's the same swallow we saw in Paris!

BULJANOFF: It is, Ninotchka! It is! He must have been in Paris! You can see it in his whole attitude! He just picked up a crumb of our black bread, shook his head, and dropped it.

[KOPALSKI: If you asked him why he left France I bet he couldn't name one good reason.

BULJANOFF: I should be a swallow! Right now I would be sitting in front of the Café de Paris picking up flakes of French pastry that would melt in my bill.

NINOTCHKA: Now, comrades . . . there is something better in life than crumbs of French pastry.

KOPALSKI *(the realist)*: Yes, a good piece of apfel strudel. . . .

NINOTCHKA: We will get that . . . we'll get everything . . . maybe a little bit later but we'll get it. . . .] We must be patient. . . . Finally we got the spring, didn't we? [We got the swallows, and you will get your apfel strudel too.

BULJANOFF *(consolingly)*: And if it is too late for you your children will eat it.]

IRANOFF *(breaking the mood)*: Let's forget the future . . . let's stop being sentimental . . . let's start that omelet.

KOPALSKI: That's right. *(He takes a little box out of his pocket)* Here's my egg. *(He hands it to* NINOTCHKA*)*

IRANOFF *unties his egg from his handkerchief.*

IRANOFF: And here's mine.

He hands it to NINOTCHKA.

BULJANOFF *reaches in his pocket and from his expression we see that a catastrophe must have happened.*

BULJANOFF: Comrades . . . I'm out of the omelet.

NINOTCHKA: Don't worry . . . there will be enough.

IRANOFF: Come, Ninotchka, let's make it in real Parisian style!

The group all go to the gas cooker and NINOTCHKA *starts to make the omelet. The others stand around as though they were watching a great event.*

KOPALSKI: Let's fill it with *confitures, des prunes* . . .

[BULJANOFF: . . . *des raisins de Madère, des framboises* . . . (. . . with grapes of Madeira, with raspberries . . .)

IRANOFF: . . . *des petites fraises des bois* . . . *de la crème de Bretagne* . . . (. . . with small wild strawberries . . . with cream . . .)

KOPALSKI: . . . so it blows up *that* big . . . what they call an Omelette Surprise!

BULJANOFF: And the surprise is there's nothing in it.

KOPALSKI: I know, but if we can't put in all these wonderful things at least let's put in some imagination. *(He raises his voice)* In that one omelet we'll taste the whole of Paris!]

The door through which GURGANOV *disappeared opens and* GURGANOV *comes out.*

IRANOFF *(seeing him)*: Sssh!

The conversation stops. GURGANOV *walks quietly through the room, again observing everything. He goes out at last.*

IRANOFF: A man like that . . . all he has to do is to walk through a room and the omelet drops.

There is a dead silence. All are again aware of the reality which surrounds. They concentrate quietly on the frying pan.

Dissolve to:

Insert of the Frying Pan

The eggs are gradually taking the shape of an omelet.

Dissolve to:
Insert of a Plate on the Table

Only the last scraps of the omelet are on it. BULJANOFF'S *hand comes in with a big piece of bread with which he sops up every fragment that is left.*

Dissolve to:
Medium Shot—Ninotchka's Room—Evening

The curtains are drawn and the lamp lighted. All four are sitting around the table, in the center of which is a samovar. In front of each of them is a glass of tea. One of the RUSSIANS *is playing a balalaika and all are singing gaily, "Paris."*

(See film still 24.)

NINOTCHKA *is enjoying their companionship. After a little while the door to the corridor opens and* NINOTCHKA'S *other roommate, the street-car conductor, strides in. She is a square-set, unfriendly woman in uniform.*

At sight of her one of the RUSSIANS *nudges* NINOTCHKA, *makes the gesture of ringing up a fare, and accompanies it with an inquiring look.* NINOTCHKA *nods. The* RUSSIANS *change their tune quickly to the "Volga Boatman" in order not to awaken animosity.*

The street-car conductor goes to her bed and starts to take off her shoes and her coat, then draws the curtain. During the following scene we hear the splash of water and the sound of gargling.

Again GURGANOV *crosses the room, this time accompanied by his little son.*

Suddenly the door is opened by VLADIMIR, *a friendly old man.*

VLADIMIR *(calling into the room)*: Comrade Yakushova, here, the postman left a letter for you.

He hands her a letter and exits.

Close Shot—Ninotchka

She takes the letter, glances at the envelope, and is stunned. She turns the envelope—an expression of breathless wonder comes over her face.

ALL THREE RUSSIANS: What is it, Ninotchka?

NINOTCHKA: It's from Paris.

IRANOFF AND BULJANOFF: From Paris?

KOPALSKI: A bill?

NINOTCHKA: From Leon.

ALL THREE RUSSIANS: From Leon! . . . How is he? . . . Come, tell us . . . open it . . . tell us . . . how is he?

NINOTCHKA sits in the chair nearest the lamp. All three are looking over her shoulder. NINOTCHKA hesitates to open the letter, obviously wanting to read it all by herself. Realizing her feelings, the THREE RUSSIANS walk to the far end of the room and sit down on a little bench, looking toward NINOTCHKA with childlike expectancy. In great anticipation NINOTCHKA opens the letter. She starts to read it. Suddenly her expression changes to one of terrific disappointment. She turns the letter over, glances at the second page, then puts the letter down on the table. The RUSSIANS have followed her expression closely. Slowly they walk over to her.

IRANOFF *(very sympathetic)*: Bad news?

NINOTCHKA: Look for yourselves.

IRANOFF picks up the letter. All three look at it.

Insert of First Page of Letter, *held in* IRANOFF's *hand. In* LEON's *handwriting we read:*

"Ninotchka, my darling,"

The rest of the writing is blocked out, line by line, and across the page is a big stamp which says "Censored." IRANOFF's *hand turns the page. The second page is also censored except for the final words,*

"*Yours, Leon.*"

Shot of the Whole Group

IRANOFF *puts the letter back on the table. They all under-stand and realize that* NINOTCHKA *wants to be alone.*

KOPALSKI: Well, I think it's getting late. Good night, Ninotchka.

IRANOFF: Thank you for a wonderful dinner.

Ninotchka rises and shakes their hands.

NINOTCHKA *(with great warmth)*: Good night, my friends.

The three start to leave but BULJANOFF *returns and whispers to* NINOTCHKA.

BULJANOFF: They can't censor our memories, can they?

NINOTCHKA *presses his hand. He walks quietly out with the others.*

NINOTCHKA, *left alone, sits down. She is heartbroken. Her thoughts are too sad and too far away to be disturbed by the snoring which comes from the corner where the street-car con-ductor has gone to bed.*

Fade out

Fade in:

Close Shot—the Window of Razinin's Office, *shooting from the inside. Through the window the background of Moscow. It is winter and snow is on the roofs. The* CAMERA PULLS BACK *and discloses* RAZININ *sitting at his desk, reading a report with a stern expression.*

107

Medium Shot—Razinin's Office

NINOTCHKA *enters carrying several folders. She walks to* RAZININ'*s desk and stands waiting for him to recognize her presence. She is a tired, stern girl.* RAZININ *looks up.*

RAZININ: Good morning, Comrade.

NINOTCHKA *(very businesslike)*: Good morning, Comrade Commissar. Here is my report on the materials available for trading in the next four months.

RAZININ: Does this include the products of the Far Eastern provinces?

NINOTCHKA: Yes, it does.

RAZININ: You mean you have finished the whole investigation?

NINOTCHKA: Yes.

RAZININ: That's marvelous. . . . You must have worked day and night. . . . Don't you ever sleep?

NINOTCHKA: I need very little sleep. We must be extremely careful what goods we take in exchange. I have already started a survey of our most urgent needs.

RAZININ: Well, Comrade, I am afraid you will have to turn over that work to someone else.

NINOTCHKA *(startled)*: May I ask why?

RAZININ: Please . . . sit down.

NINOTCHKA *sits.*

RAZININ: Cigarette?

NINOTCHKA: Thank you.

RAZININ: Well, Comrade, have you heard from your friends Kopalski, Buljanoff, and Iranoff?

NINOTCHKA: No.

RAZININ: I haven't either, but I've heard *about* them. You must realize it was only on the strength of your Paris report that I sent them to Constantinople; without that I never would have trusted them on a mission as important as the fur deal.

NINOTCHKA: May I ask what has happened?

RAZININ: As soon as our representatives go to a foreign country they seem to lose all sense of balance. If I told you what's going on in Constantinople right now you wouldn't believe it. Those three have been sitting there for six weeks and haven't sold a piece of fur. *(He points to the folder)* This anonymous report was sent me. They are dragging the good name of our country through every café and night club. Here . . . *(He reads from the report)* "How can the Bolshevik cause gain respect among the Moslems if your three representatives, Buljanoff, Iranoff, and Kopalski, get so drunk that they throw a carpet out of their hotel window and complain to the management that it didn't fly?"

NINOTCHKA *has to suppress a smile of amusement at the antics of her three old friends.*

NINOTCHKA: Oh, they shouldn't do such things. Are you sure this report is correct?

RAZININ: It gives details which couldn't be invented. Naturally I want to verify it and that's why I need you.

NINOTCHKA *(apprehensively)*: You want me to go to Constantinople?

RAZININ: Yes . . . leaving immediately.

NINOTCHKA *(her one object to escape the mission)*: I appreciate the confidence you show in me, but I must ask you to entrust someone else with this mission. I should hate to interrupt my present work. I am positive that my survey is more important than finding out whether three of our comrades have been drinking some extra glasses of champagne.

RAZININ *(austerely)*: That is for me to decide, Comrade Yakushova.

NINOTCHKA: I am sorry, I don't want to overstep my position— but please . . . don't send me.

RAZININ: I don't understand.

NINOTCHKA *(making a last effort)*: How can I make myself clear. . . . It is difficult to express but I'd rather not go to foreign countries any more. Please, Comrade . . . let me stay here . . . let me finish my work. . . . I am in the rhythm of it now . . . I don't want to go away. I don't want to be sent into that foreign atmosphere again. It throws one out of gear. . . . Let me finish my work . . . I have concentrated everything in it. . . . Please . . . don't make me go.

RAZININ: Please don't waste my time, Comrade. Do your duty. Good-by.

NINOTCHKA: I will do my best.

She exits, as we

Dissolve to:

Establishing Shot of Constantinople, *on a bright sunlit day, if possible with the circling shadow of an airplane.*

Dissolve to:

Long Shot—Airport in Constantinople, *shooting from an airplane angle. A crowd is awaiting the arrival of a plane. The* CAMERA *goes down to a* CLOSE SHOT *of* BULJANOFF, IRANOFF, *and* KOPALSKI, *standing in the crowd.*

All three are very elegantly and gaily dressed. They are in the happiest mood. One of them carries a large bouquet of flowers to greet NINOTCHKA.

Dissolve to:

Living Room of a Very Luxurious Hotel Suite *in Constantinople. Its style should suggest the locale.* NINOTCHKA *enters with the* THREE RUSSIANS, *who are very happy to have her with them again.*

KOPALSKI *(indicating the room)*: How do you like it, Ninotchka? Isn't it wonderful?

IRANOFF and BULJANOFF: Tell us . . . tell us.

NINOTCHKA *protests, but during the whole scene it is evident*

110

that behind her protestations there is none of the force and conviction she displayed in a similar situation in the Royal Suite.

NINOTCHKA: But Buljanoff, Iranoff, Kopalski . . .

IRANOFF: Now, please, Ninotchka, don't start figuring it out in cows.

NINOTCHKA: You've done it again and I am responsible. How can you forget yourselves this way? You were sent here to make money, not to spend it.

(See film still 25.)

IRANOFF: Buljanoff, she still has those old-fashioned Bolshevik ideas.

BULJANOFF: It is high time you got out of Russia.

NINOTCHKA *(not knowing what to do with the three rascals)*: I must be stern with you.

KOPALSKI *(delighted)*: That's our old Ninotchka!

BULJANOFF and IRANOFF *(agreeing with him)*: Yes, yes.

NINOTCHKA: Don't forget, the day will come when you will have to face Razinin.

BULJANOFF *(cockily)*: Good old Razinin! Is he still alive? How does he manage?

NINOTCHKA: But, Comrades . . .

KOPALSKI *(with the happiness of being free again in his voice)*: We are not comrades any more . . . we are friends, Ninotchka.

BULJANOFF: Imagine, we don't have to whisper any longer.

IRANOFF: We can say whatever we want. We can shout . . . we can complain. . . . Look . . . *(He opens the door leading to corridor)* The service in this hotel is terrible! *(He closes the door)* See? Nobody comes . . . nobody pays any attention. That's freedom.

BULJANOFF *(dryly)*: No, that's bad management.

NINOTCHKA: Is it possible to bring you back to reality for a moment? I must have a complete report of your negotiations and a detailed expense account.

BULJANOFF: Don't ask for it, Ninotchka. There is a Turkish proverb which says, "If something smells bad, why put your nose in it?"

NINOTCHKA: And there is a Russian saying: "The cat who has cream on his whiskers had better find good excuses."

BULJANOFF: With our cream situation what it is, it is Russia which should apologize to the cats.

[NINOTCHKA *(helplessly)*: Friends . . . friends, Buljanoff, Iranoff . . .

KOPALSKI *(afraid of being left out)*: . . . and Kopalski.

NINOTCHKA *(pleadingly)*: Don't make it difficult for me. This is no more a pleasure trip for me than it is for you.

IRANOFF: That was our idea when we first came. All we thought we would get out of this trip was a Turkish bath, but . . . we learned better.

KOPALSKI: Ninotchka, we are in the magic East, the country of Aladdin and His Lamp . . .

IRANOFF: . . . Ali Baba and the Forty Thieves . . . into one single hour you can crowd a thousand and one nights.

BULJANOFF: All you have to do is say "open sesame."]

NINOTCHKA: I don't know how I can get you out of it this time. How will it end? What will happen to you?

BULJANOFF *(intimately)*: Shall we tell her?

IRANOFF and KOPALSKI: Yes.

BULJANOFF *(proudly)*: Ninotchka, I hope you'll be our guest.

NINOTCHKA: Guest?

BULJANOFF: We have opened a restaurant. . . .

IRANOFF: . . . we have a wonderful electric sign: "Dine With Buljanoff, Iranoff, and Kopalski."

NINOTCHKA: You mean you are deserting Russia?

KOPALSKI *(singing the song of freedom)*: Don't call it desertion. Our little restaurant . . . that is our Russia . . . the Russia of borscht, the Russia of beef Stroganoff, blinis with sour cream . . .

112

IRANOFF: . . . the Russia of piroshki . . . people will eat and love it.

BULJANOFF: We are not only serving good food, we are serving our country . . . we are making friends.

NINOTCHKA *(completely bewildered)*: Who gave you this idea? What is responsible for all this?

KOPALSKI *(with a gleam in his eye)*: There's something in Constantinople . . . something irresistible. . . .

IRANOFF: . . . it is in the air . . . it may come around the corner as you walk down the street. . . .

BULJANOFF: . . . it may step out of a bazaar . . . it may wait for you in a corridor . . . it may hide in the shadow of a minaret. . . .

KOPALSKI *(pointing to the balcony)*: Right now it's on the balcony.

NINOTCHKA *looks toward the balcony and is dumbfounded as she sees* LEON *standing there smiling at her. He walks quietly toward her.*

LEON *(looking longingly at* NINOTCHKA*)*: They wouldn't let me in so I had to get you out.

NINOTCHKA *(still taken aback)*: So—you're behind all this. I should have known.

LEON *takes her hand and kisses it. The* THREE RUSSIANS *exchange glances. The* CAMERA PANS WITH THEM—*leaving* NINOTCHKA *and* LEON *as* RUSSIANS *walk discreetly out of the room and close the door behind them.*

Close Shot—Leon and Ninotchka

LEON: Trying to keep me away from you! It couldn't be done. Naturally I couldn't go on forever punching passport officials in the nose—but I found a way, didn't I? Darling, I had to see you. I wrote and wrote but all my letters came back.

NINOTCHKA: The one I got they wouldn't let me read. *(Carried away by emotion)* It began, "Ninotchka, my darling," and ended, "Yours, Leon."

113

LEON (*with great feeling and sincerity*): I won't tell you what came between . . . I'll prove it. It will take a long time, Ninotchka . . . at least a lifetime.

NINOTCHKA *is aware that she is facing a decision. She knows what she wants but still tries to evade a definite answer.*

NINOTCHKA: But, Leon, I am only here for a few days.

LEON: If you don't stay with me, I'll have to continue my fight. I'll travel wherever Russian commissions are. I'll turn them all into Buljanoffs, Iranoffs, and Kopalskis. The world will be crowded with Russian restaurants. I'll depopulate Russia. Once you saved your country by going back. This time you can save it by staying here.

NINOTCHKA: Well, when it is a choice between my personal interest and the good of my country, how can I waver? No one shall say Ninotchka was a bad Russian.[37]

LEON *takes her in his arms, they kiss* [as we

(See film still 26.)

Fade out][38]

The End

[37] In the film, LEON says, "Darling!"
[38] In the film, we see a sign which reads:

DINE WITH
BULJANOFF
IRANOFF
& KOPALSKI

The camera pulls back to show people eating in front of the restaurant, others walking past on the sidewalk. Kopalski is picketing the place, wearing a sign which reads:

BULJANOFF
AND
IRANOFF
UNFAIR TO
KOPALSKI

He starts to turn about. "The End" fades in and out.